From Connectivity to Community

The ICF Method for economic, social and cultural growth in the digital age

By Robert Bell
With John Jung and Louis Zacharilla

Published by
Intelligent Community Forum

First edition, published by Intelligent Community Forum
250 Park Avenue, 7th Floor, New York, NY 10177 USA
www.intelligentcommunity.org

The City of Hamilton's experience in working with the Intelligent Community Forum (ICF) has been nothing short of spectacular. From learning best practices from cities across the globe to the rich networking opportunities to working with the wonderful ICF team, Hamilton has benefitted greatly.

- **Mayor Fred Eisenberger, Hamilton, Ontario, Canada**

ICF thinking and your six success Factors have propelled Hudson, Ohio into the future. Your success factors gave us both a language and a yardstick. Over the last four years, we have deepened our relationships with virtually all of our key community partners and they have fostered great success. Our work with the ICF has given us a head start.

- **Jane Howington, City Manager, Hudson, Ohio, USA**

Through the ICF process, we are excited to benefit from the learnings of other global cities and to serve as a leading example to municipalities locally, and abroad, who are looking to start, or enhance their efforts to become more intelligent, liveable and vibrant communities.

- **Mayor Frank Scarpitti, Markham, Ontario, Canada**

Espoo's strategy, *The Espoo Story*, states that we want to be Europe's most sustainable city – not only ecologically but also economically, socially and culturally. The ICF Method recognizes the key factors to achieve that: engaging people, boosting innovation and putting new technologies to work, while making sure no one is left behind.

- **Päivi Sutinen, Director, City as Service Development, Espoo, Finland**

The ICF Method presents cities with a strong framework to view their communities from six key Factors that are vital to ensuring a focus on relevant elements to better position them to succeed in an increasingly competitive economic development environment.

- **Dayna Spiring, President & CEO, Economic Development Winnipeg, Manitoba, Canada**

For our region, being an Intelligent Community embraces all that's important to our residents, not just what's happening in the economic or technological front, but key learnings and bright futures for our young people and the enhancement of a healthy, smart and creative community. It ensures that we keep the citizens at the heart of our decision-making process.

- **Mayor Mark Jamieson, Sunshine Coast, Queensland, Australia**

The ICF process for us was a process of discovery. By framing our story around the six development Factors, we were able to discover things going on in our own community which we weren't even fully aware of. We discovered certain common commitments and core values of innovation that trace back to our city's founding. Through participation in the annual Summit, we discovered in talking to other cities that what we are doing here in Westerville truly is unique.

- **Todd Jackson, Chief Information Officer, Westerville, Ohio, USA**

Table of Contents

How to Use this Book

From Connectivity to Community was written to help communities – including the small-to-midsize ones that make up the majority – develop the broadband and digital assets that the modern economy demands and to turn them into inclusive prosperity and social and cultural growth.

That's a lot of ideas packed into one sentence, so let's say it again. Growth in your local economy, in the social richness of your community and in its traditions and culture are the things that make a community worth living in. It is what attracts outsiders to settle there, what keeps people and employers from moving away, and what makes possible every other thing we love about the place called home. As we will explain later, those things are under siege all over the world from massive waves of change in the economy, in society and in culture generated, as tidal waves are born from undersea earthquakes, by technology change. This book is your guide to a new approach to economic development that will enable your community to adapt, survive and thrive amid the storm.

If you are looking for advice on becoming a Smart City, you will find some of that here. But Smart City stuff is, frankly, just tinkering around the edges of the big, hairy, inescapable challenges of our time. Mastering a few technology tricks to make your municipality or county run better is good. But it is not going to change lives for the better. It will not create employment or drive inclusive growth. It will not keep the brightest youth from leaving town for greener pastures. It will not give birth to the next generation of employers or ensure that your people have the skills needed to work for them. You may start your journey with a Smart City project, but we hope you will notch up much greater achievements before the end.

Who are we writing for? For community leaders in local governments and regional districts. For members of legislatures, educators, technology providers, business leaders, agencies, economic development and regional planning organizations. For people who care deeply about the future of the place called home and are willing to take action to make it a successful one.

What to Expect

In these pages, you will find:

- A new method for economic development in the digital age, which aims to create a lasting foundation for broad-based prosperity while supporting social and cultural growth – and drawing on it for greater economic vitality.
- Examples of communities that grew their economies, addressed social challenges, strengthened community bonds and enriched their culture.
- Roadmaps that show six Factors for the development of your community by improving its people's skills, making businesses more innovative and successful, using technology to better serve people, and contributing to the spirit that makes the community unique.

About the Intelligent Community Forum

From *Connectivity to Community* was developed by the Intelligent Community Forum, based on two decades of research, consultation and education. Today, the Forum is a global movement of cities, metro regions and counties with a think tank at its heart. ICF studies and promotes the best practices of the world's Intelligent Communities as they adapt to the new demands and seize the opportunities presented by information and communications technology (ICT). To help cities and regions build prosperous economies, solve social problems and enrich local cultures, the Intelligent Community Forum publishes research, hosts global events, licenses institutes and national organizations to carry on its work and produces an annual international awards program.

In 2012 ICF was invited to participate at the Nobel Peace Prize conference in Oslo and in 2014, its model was recognized by the U.S. Department of Commerce under the Workforce Innovation and Opportunity Act. According to the American government, ICF's work is "aimed at creating a more flexible and responsive system of workforce development to meet the needs of employers looking to fill 21st Century jobs."

For more information:

Web: www.intelligentcommunity.org.

Twitter: @newcommunities

LinkedIn Group: Intelligent Community Forum

Facebook Page: Intelligent Community Forum

Welcome to the Digital Economy – and Good Luck!

We are living through a time when technology is changing history. It is not the first time. But learning about history in a classroom or museum is one thing. Living through it is another.

For us, the explosion of *digital connectivity,* and the *digital applications* that run on it, knows no parallel. Carrying a supercomputer in your pocket or handbag – and having it connected to devices belonging to billions of others – has turned the world upside down.

A Tale of Tech Giants

Just consider the story of three of today's Tech Giants.

Facebook started life as a project in a campus dorm room. Just 14 years later, the company had 2 billion users and earned $30 billion in revenue. That's utterly impossible. *Impossible.* Yet it happened. In the process, it has created new markets and jobs, and has minted enormous wealth for some – while also driving competing companies into extinction and sparking growing concerns about privacy and the power of unregulated online media to foster hate, create division and undermine democracy.

14 years

The biggest hotel company in the world is not Hilton, Marriott or Hyatt. It is Airbnb. Only ten years after its founding in 2008, it was offering over 4 million listings in 65,000 cities, and analysts

Airbnb

estimated its total value at $32 billion. All without owning any of the property it brings to market, which it does entirely through the internet and a mobile app. It has given property owners new ways to generate income. It has also brought unwelcome crowding and noise to many neighborhoods and may be worsening the problem of homelessness.

The world's biggest retailer does not – unlike Walmart, Tesco or Carrefour – own any of the inventory it sells. It is the Chinese company Alibaba, which operates a 100% online marketplace connecting buyers and sellers. It was founded in 1999, taking its name from a character in the *Arabian Nights*. Just nineteen years later, it earned $39 billion from a platform used by 550 million customers. It has made e-commerce available to millions of businesses – and driven quite a few of them under.

Alibaba

Numbers like these give us a sense of the scope and scale of the change. To understand its sheer power, you need only look at your own life. It is all but impossible to apply for a job that pays a living wage unless you do it online. Your children will fall behind in school unless they can use the internet to do their homework. We worry about screen time and phone addiction, cyberbullying and revenge porn. Your digital life can be locked up by ransomware and bad attempts at humor on social media can cost you your job and your reputation. It's a bizarre world the Tech Giants have created – with our eager assistance – and its impact run deeper than most of us can imagine.

A Tale of Two Economies

Six decades ago, a famed Finnish architect named Alvar Aalto built a red-brick paper mill in Hamina, a town of 20,000 in southeastern Finland. It closed its doors in 2008, victim of competition from much lower-cost countries. The next year, however, it was bought by Google, which transformed it into a data center. More than 2,000 people working for 50 different companies contributed to the project, which employs 125 people in full-time and contractor roles in engineering, technical work, security, food service and maintenance.

That's the positive news from the digital economy. But the story has a dark side as well.

In 2015, the three biggest Tech Giants – Apple, Facebook and Google – generated $1 trillion in sales and employed 137,000 people. Compare that to 1990, when the three biggest automakers – GM, Ford and Chrysler – generated US$65 billion in sales (measured in 2015 dollars). To do it, they employed a bit more than *one million people.*

Those two sets of numbers tell the story of economic disruption wrought by digital technologies. The biggest growth businesses of the 21st Century employ a paltry number of people per dollar or euro or yen or renminbi earned, compared with the growth industries of yesterday. Going a step further, many of the high-growth Tech Giants are doing more than that. In the US, visits to shopping malls fell 50% from 2010 to 2013 and have fallen every year since. Even before COVID19 lockdowns decimated retailing, department stores had lost 18 times more workers than coal mining since 2001.[1]

Why? E-commerce, of course, led by Tech Giant Amazon, which accounted for 44% of all US e-commerce sales in 2017.[2] Worldwide e-commerce sales more than doubled to $2.8 trillion from 2014 to 2018.[3] E-commerce is expected to become the largest retail sales channel in the world by 2021.[4] The upside, according to economist Michael Mandel, is that e-commerce has created 355,000 new jobs in the warehouses, shipping and other back-office work. Those new jobs pay better than traditional retail jobs and wages are growing fast. But they also require more education than is typical for retail workers, which spells trouble for most. [5]

These changes are creating two economies, which offer completely different experiences to those inside them. Call them the Gold Economy and the Copper Economy.

In the Gold Economy, workers find good jobs in growth industries like information technology and digital services as well as finance, advanced manufacturing and the upper levels of healthcare and government. They add big value to their employers, whether measured in profit, productivity or effectiveness, and get paid good wages in return. They can afford to live in prosperous neighborhoods that offer attractive retail, strong schools and rewarding social and cultural institutions. They complain about the unrelenting pace of work – running faster and faster just to keep up – but they also reap the gold.

Copper is useful stuff. We couldn't live without it to carry electricity, communications and water. But it's also what pennies are made of, at least in the United States. In the Copper Economy, workers are stuck in menial jobs that generate only small value for their employers. That keeps their wages low. They work in food services and accommodation, transportation, domestic service, manual healthcare and social services, building administration and waste services. They live paycheck-to-paycheck in places with poor housing, limited and costly retail outlets and too little in the way of culture or entertainment.

They have something else in common, too. They probably do not live in the Copper Economy by accident. They are more likely to be members of minority groups that have felt the sharp end of racism for generations, if not centuries. Their grandparents and parents and they themselves are more likely to have been actively discriminated against throughout their lives in employment, education, housing and voting. They are Black and Native and Latino Americans. They are Black Brazilians or South Africans, the Aborigines of Australia and Maori of New Zealand, the Dalit of India, the Rohingya of Myanmar and the descendants of Turkish guest workers in Germany and Arab immigrants in France.

The death of George Floyd under the knee of an American police officer in 2020 was a uniquely American event, tied as it was to centuries of slavery and its extension by unjust laws and racism embedded in American culture. Yet protests in George Floyd's name sprang up all around the world – because the denial of opportunity, equality and humanity to minorities is a universal sin.

The awakening to injustice, whether momentary or lasting, adds weight to the fundamental questions facing every municipality and region in the world. How can your local economy be more Golden than Coppery – and how widely will the gold be shared? This is the question to which the rest of this book is devoted.

The Toll of Machine Intelligence

And if you think this question matters today, you ain't seen nothing yet.

The rise of machine learning and artificial intelligence is expected to replace many of the job functions that humans currently perform. While few categories of employment will disappear altogether, artificial intelligence will drive decline in some jobs and disruption in many more. [6]

About 5% of occupations could have close to 100% of their tasks automated

- Sewing machine operators
- Assembly line workers
- Motor vehicle operators
- Warehouse workers

About 60% of occupations could have 30% of their tasks automated

- Office and administrative staff
- Management and business operations
- Web developers
- Nursing assistants

The storm of disruption in the economy will eventually ease, as it always has. We will go through a period of adaptation and absorption, as we learn to make our digital tools serve us more than we are forced serve them. But in the meantime, every community faces a choice. The challenges are great but so are the opportunities to produce a future more promising than the past. For all the disruption brought by technology, it also offers new hope.

For three thousand years, we have only known one way to spark economic growth and the social and cultural growth that follows it: to concentrate a large number of people in a small geographic area called a city, so they can do business, exchange knowledge, invent new things and amass new wealth. Today, the United Nations forecasts a continued rise in the economic prospects of the world's developing nations – and that has led in a straight line to forecasts that most of the world's people will live in megacities, from Tokyo and New York to Jakarta, Delhi, Manila, Sao Paulo, Bangkok and Kolkata.

The flip side of that forecast is a massive depopulation of everywhere else – economic decline, social breakdown and cultural poverty – together with a rise of urban ills in the megacities, from congestion and pollution to inequality and homelessness.

It doesn't have to be that way.

Distributed Development

Digital technologies are already making it possible for people with the right skills to earn their living almost anywhere. They are a tiny minority of the population today but where those individuals go today, companies will follow. They are following now. Even very small companies today may have employees spread across countries and around the world.

By its nature, digital tech is *distributive*. It does not require centralization of people and resources. It encourages the creation of many hubs of talent, expertise and market access, and by networking them together, creates a virtual whole much greater than the sum of the individual parts. It opens a path for the midsize and even small city to chart an independent economic destiny that preserves what its people love most about it while creating the future they dream about.

It will not make the big city obsolete – indeed, so far, it is hastening the concentration of talent in urban cores. But it opens a new path for small-to-midsize cities to build the same kind of economic, social and cultural dynamism found in the world's leading cities. On a different scale, certainly. Lacking the crazy energy, the masking anonymity and the apparently bottomless potential of the big city. But possessing attributes just as valuable: a human scale, lower costs of living, ease of getting around, more natural beauty in most cases, and generally a much easier time getting things done.

We know that it is possible, that it is happening now, because we follow the cities that are doing it. Places like the Sunshine Coast in Queensland, Australia and Whanganui in New Zealand. Like Chattanooga, Tennessee and Mitchell, South Dakota in the US. Or Waterloo, Ontario and Abbotsford, British Columbia in Canada, or Eindhoven, Netherlands or Espoo, Finland. These are places you have probably never heard of, but where the future of our world is being written.

That future had already become clear before the COVID19 pandemic gave the world another reason not to concentrate too much economic activity in a few big places. Social distancing – the only proven way to keep infectious diseases under control – demonstrated with shocking suddenness the power of broadband to enable economic, social and cultural activity. It substituted for classroom education, for conferences, for customer meetings and happy hour socializing. Admittedly, it did none of these things really well. That's hardly surprising, since this was our first experience at making serious use of its capabilities. But there was no avoiding the lesson: geographic dispersion coupled with connectivity can offer an extra layer of resilience in the face of threats, whether they are natural disasters or terrorist attacks.

The path to true distributed development is not easy or quick. For each of these cities and hundreds more, it has taken vision, an engaged community, strong leadership and the willingness to play the long game. But the model they have proven is available to any city, town, country or region willing to start the journey and stick to the road. And the first step, as an economic development leader of a small city once told us, doesn't cost a thing. The first step is to change your mind.

The ICF Method

The ICF Method dates from our first studies of communities wrestling with the challenges looming on the horizon of the digital revolution. Over the past 20 years, it has been refined and improved by their experiences and has shaped the analytic tools we use to track them.

The Method is a way to *think differently* about the economic, social and cultural future of the place called home. It asks the leadership of communities to be both *visionary* – imagining previously impossible outcomes – and *practical*, adding new items to their long priority lists and ensuring that these things get done.

We do not usually talk about economic, social and economic growth in the same breath. Making money is making money: what can it have to do with the rest? But a moment's thought makes clear that a healthy economy is the necessary condition for a healthy society and an active culture that looks not just to the past but expresses optimism about the future. When the money runs out, it's hard for the people of a community to hang together. When they do, it is mostly in opposition to the outside world that has done them wrong, and the culture they share looks backward to better times, real or imagined, instead of forward. Economic, social and cultural health are the three pillars on which a good quality of life depends, one that makes the community a great place to live, work, start a business, raise a family and guide the next generation to maturity. Take away any one of them, and the foundation begins to crumble.

THE ICF METHOD

Six Factors that impact economic, social and cultural growth

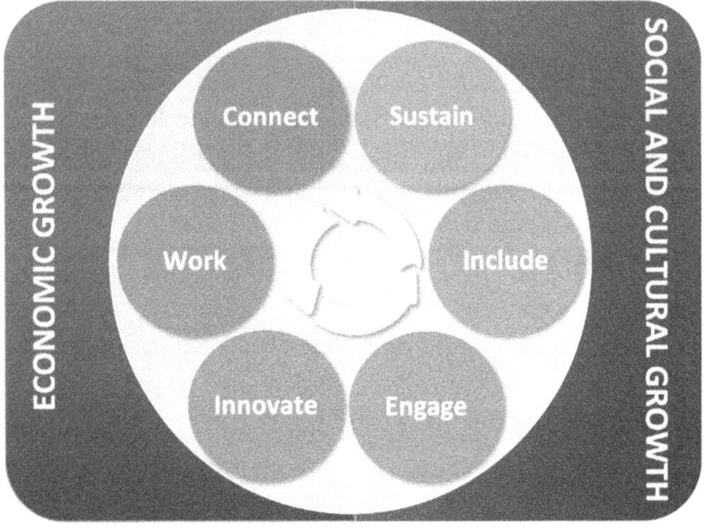

© 2019 Intelligent Community Forum

The core idea behind the Method is that there is a new way to conduct economic development in the digital age, which produces much greater success and also strengthens the social and cultural pillars of the community. It consists of six Factors that contribute to that virtuous cycle. Three of them drive growth in the economy, which powers every other thing of value in a community. Three of them are about caring for the community as it grows. They sustain its growth and manage the inevitable bad effects it brings, so as to preserve the quality of life that means so much to the people who live there and help attract and retain talented people and the organizations who employ them.

CONNECT High-speed connections for computers and mobile devices are the infrastructure no community can do without. Through those connections come employment opportunities, education, commerce, information, entertainment and community participation. Businesses depend on them to manage their operations, reach customers and attract employees. Governments rely on them to generate and analyze massive amounts of data to improve decision-making. Citizens use them to organize and coordinate, share ideas and build community spirit. Connected digital infrastructure including sensors and cameras make possible machine learning and Internet of Things (IoT) applications that deliver better services for less money to more people and organizations.

WORK The well-paying work of the 21st Century is knowledge work. All opportunity for rewarding employment has shifted to those with skills, from the construction trades and work in automated factories to teaching, technology, finance and business management. Those without the right skills are increasingly being left behind. Intelligent Communities create a knowledge-based workforce through strong and continuing collaboration among local government, employers and schools. Together, they turn education into a ladder of opportunity that teaches skills that are in demand and connects young people with opportunities in the region to strengthen the community's economic and social foundation.

INNOVATE The economist Robert Solow won the Nobel Prize in 1987 for proving that 80% of all economic growth comes from developing and using new technology. That's a stunning number. It means that if your employers, institutions and government are not creating new opportunities or putting new technology to work, you are missing out on 80% of the potential growth in today's economy. That's why every place needs an innovation strategy, which may range from tech clubs and hackathons to startup districts and IoT infrastructure.

ENGAGE You can only create positive change in a community with the permission of that community. People may not yet understand the challenges or have any idea how to tackle them. But they can become either the biggest obstacle to positive change or its most powerful advocates. Engaging people in the earliest stages of projects creates ownership. Ensuring that projects are designed and executed in a transparent and ethical manner builds trust. More than ever before, residents have digital tools at their disposal for developing coalitions, coordinating action and turning the fears or enthusiasms of a few people into a community-wide movement. That can drive your strategy forward or freeze it in its tracks.

INCLUDE The explosive advance of the digital economy has worsened the exclusion of people who already play a peripheral role in the economy and society, whether due to poverty, lack of education, prejudice, age, disability or location. It has also disrupted industries from manufacturing to retail services, enlarging the number of people for whom the digital revolution is a burden rather than a blessing. Effective digital inclusion programs target access to technology and services, the issues of affordability and motivation to use digital technology and learn digital skills.

SUSTAIN

Climate change is the single biggest threat – and opportunity – facing our world and communities. The threat is obvious to all, except for those who work hard *not* to understand it. The opportunity lies in our response. Working on sustainability has the power to energize community groups, neighborhoods and community leaders with the promise of making a difference. They work they do in collaboration with government can have tangible impact on local quality of life, making people prouder of the place they live. Sustainability is also about economic growth. As the world slowly begins reining in human impact on the planet, sustainability is generating substantial new opportunities for technology advance, business growth and employment in green industries.

* * * * *

These six Factors are *interdependent*: the success of each tends to support the success of the others. They are powerful in very large cities but even more so in *small-to-midsize* places, because change can come more easily when there are fewer key people and constituencies who must change their minds. They require *resources* but are also implemented one step at a time, so that each successful step helps produce more resources for the next.

More than any other requirement, they demand that you *get started.* Planning is necessary. Meetings must take place and coalitions must be built. But the ICF Method is a series of experiments guided by experience. It is not until the first experiment is underway that your journey truly begins.

Is an Intelligent Community Just a Smart City?

You probably know what a Smart City is. But what is an Intelligent Community? Do we really need another word for the same old thing?

We don't – but then, it is *not* the same old thing. Since IBM coined the term and Cisco quickly followed its lead, there have been, according to the web, three generations of smart cities. There have been academic papers and workshops and massive conferences. Multinational, national and local programs have poured billions into projects. Technologies have been developed to improve how cities manage everything from energy, water, public safety and pollution to transportation, healthcare and tax collection. Consultants have prospered, IT systems sales have grown and CIOs have earned new respect. Now, after more than two decades of smart cities adoption, what do we have to show for all that investment?

Frankly, not much.

It's Not the Technology

Not that there's anything wrong with the technology. It's like automating a factory. Install the sensors, cameras, computers and network connections across the municipality. Integrate them all with software, big data and artificial intelligence. Better data leads to better decisions, and automation lets you do more with less labor. It's a win for the city, its residents and taxpayers.

It's just very much of a win.

We get a 5% increase in efficiency, a 10% reduction in costs, a 30% drop in time wasted looking for a parking spot. Wow. We do also sometimes save lives thanks to more efficient policing, firefighting and emergency response. But, according to a 2017 analysis by Statista, only 11% of smart city spending worldwide goes toward public safety.

So, aside from saving those lives, what difference have smart cities made to their citizens? Are they enjoying more freedom, more opportunity, greater prosperity or stronger connection to the community and its culture because they live in a smart city? Is there greater and fairer access to education? Are the great disparities in household wealth smaller? Have we improved access to housing or attacked the root causes of crime?

That might seem a long and unfair wish list to burden smart cities with. But if we're going to spend billions, shouldn't it be on **something that matters**?

It Starts with Good Jobs

For all of its cool technology, the Smart City movement has completely ignored the single most important contributor to a community's quality of life: widespread employment that pays well and offers new opportunity to each generation. Employment alone will not make a great place to live, but it is what makes possible everything else.

In the digital age, employment is under siege. Any line of work that pays a living wage demands a good basic education, "hard" skills needed in specific industries, the "soft" skills of the workplace and access to digital technology. To be successful, the companies that employ those workers need continuous innovation, market knowledge, adaptability and access to digital technology. And none of this stands still. The bar continuously rises for people and organizations due to the competitive acceleration brought by digital technology across global markets. Those who fail to keep up are lost to stagnation, decline and impoverishment. We see the results all around us in an economy divided into "haves" and "have-nots" – whether people, communities or entire regions – with all the social, cultural and political destruction it creates. The big challenges of today arise from rapid technology change – but to those challenges the technologists of the smart city have no answer.

A proper answer requires a new approach to developing inclusive prosperity, social health and cultural richness at the local level. Put another way, it requires a new approach to *economic development*, the critical task of promoting the creation of high-quality employment that generates prosperity. Local and state governments spend large sums every year on developing leads, cultivating relationships, crafting location or investment offers and providing incentives. These traditional practices, however, struggle to keep up with the changes in the economy, because companies seeking a location these days need more than cheap dirt, cheap labor and adequate transportation. As McKinsey partner Susan Lund put it in a paper on globalization, "Our picture of globalization is the offshoring of manufacturing jobs. But increasingly, only a small share of goods is traded globally. Low wages are no longer the driving force in global trade. If low wages aren't important to companies, what is? R&D, innovation, a skilled workforce and a start-up ecosystem."

Only rarely does this combination spring up on its own – it requires conscious cultivation over many years. The ICF Method provides the framework, specific strategies and real-world examples that communities of all sizes need to pursue this new approach to economic development in the digital age.

Start with People

The next-to-last chapter of this book ("Getting Started") offers practical steps for beginning your Intelligent Community journey: forming working groups, developing analyses, building public support and so on. Before you can start the journey, however, you need to understand what you are trying to achieve.

There are six Factors, each unique and yet each connecting with and supporting the others. Where does it make most sense to start?

You start with people.

Engage

Citizen engagement is the glue that binds Intelligent Communities to a better future. It is the deliberate effort through civic leadership to help citizens, business, institutions and community leaders understand the need for change, identify opportunities and become champions of that change.

Successful engagement provides the foundation for the community's public identity in its outreach to the world. It energizes economic development, investment attraction and business generation, because the community has built a unique vision of its character and its future. In their own eyes, its people are no longer just living in one community among hundreds of thousands like it. They are in the best place to live, work, start a business, raise a family and pass their heritage to the next generation.

Much of the work of engagement will sound familiar to community leaders: surveys and focus groups, public consultation and working groups. Intelligent Communities make sure to use digital tools as well to engage the many people unlikely to attend a public meeting. They also insist that "consultation" not be a one-way road from government to citizen. Instead, they want plans to be based on the priorities of the people and organizations in the community, so that residents see their concerns reflected in the plans that emerge. Engagement ultimately means more than participation: it means building a vision of the future in collaboration with the community and creating advocates for that future who persuade their friends and neighbors of its importance.

Engagement Looks Like:

- Government convening citizens, businesses and institutions, then facilitating and turning ideas into specific strategies and plans and, finally, marshalling resources to carry them forward.
    - Public discussion forums and brainstorming to fully understand and appreciate the challenges and opportunities facing the community.
    - Physical meetings and digital interaction to ensure the broadest possible participation.
- Government, citizens, businesspeople and nonprofit leaders engaging in projects that produce change.
- Building on early successes, continuously raising community confidence in its ability to do things that once seemed impossible.

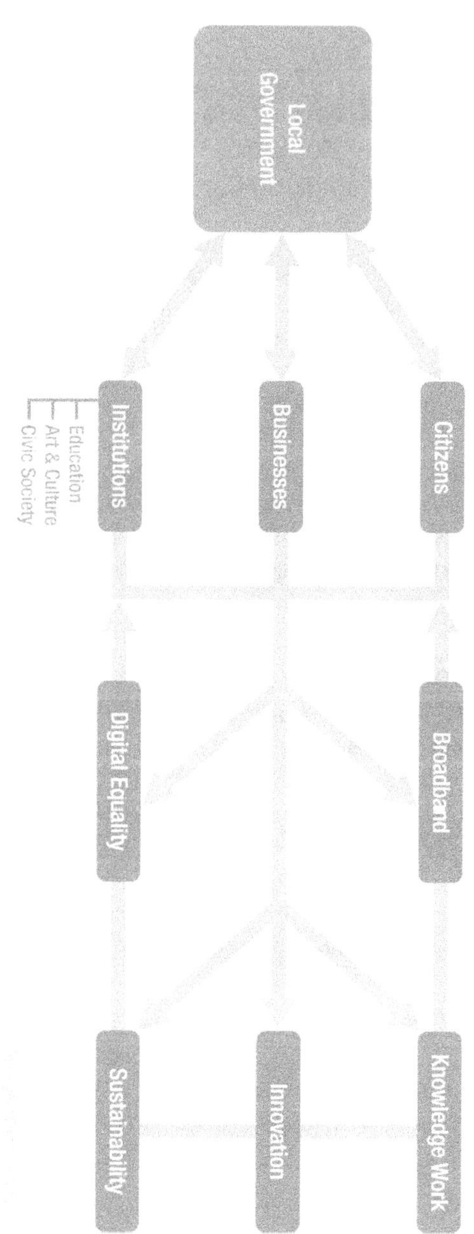
Local Government
Institutions
Education
Art & Culture
Civic Society
Businesses
Citizens
Digital Equality
Broadband
Sustainability
Innovation
Knowledge Work

COMMUNITY PROFILE

Whanganui, New Zealand

Pop: 43,600 I Top7 Intelligent Community 2017

Whanganui is located on the southwest coast of New Zealand's North Island. Bypassed by national rail lines in the 19th Century, it was bypassed again by broadband providers in the 20th. Realizing that no incumbent would help, in January 2010 the Wanganui District Council launched construction of a fiber-to-the-premise network. But they also realized that a fiber buildout was only part of the story – they needed buy-in.

They formed the Whanganui Digital Leaders Forum (WDLF), which in turn created the Wanganui Innovation Network (WIN). WIN's goals were to build awareness of digital opportunities, connect early leaders and market Whanganui as New Zealand's most progressive city.

Doing Business

WIN kicked off with an information session for 150 members of the city's business community. WDLF ran a series of speaker sessions as part of another new event, TechEx, which ran three years. Attended by 10,000 people, TechEx drew national attention.

The City built a 'Digital Whanganui' website as an online directory of local digital services and products. Digital Journey is an online hub which assists businesses to gain an understanding of the opportunities online technology offers.

Cultural Advocacy

Whanganui is mindful of keeping the local Maori indigenous community involved in its digital strategies. It has established an Innovation Quarter: a hub of collaboration where corporate, local businesses, educators and local artists and specialists interact and form strategic partnerships. A key component is the Maori

Business Hub, which creates opportunities for local Maori businesses to network with each other across a range of industries.

This combination of programs and outreach drew broad-based support from all corners of the community to support the broadband build and create demand for it across the economy.

COMMUNITY PROFILE

Westerville, Ohio, USA

Pop: 39,700 I Top7 Intelligent Community 2019

Most Intelligent Communities have a crisis in their recent past – loss of major employers, a natural disaster or environmental problem – that spurs new thinking, engagement and action. Westerville is among the handful that lacks a crisis story. Its "secret sauce" is a government culture that – driven by a "healthy paranoia" about the future – constantly communicates with people, businesses and institutions to identify new needs. Then they make targeted investments ahead of actual demand, and these create opportunities.

Uptown

That spirit is evident in the historic Uptown business district. Designated a landmark, it is full of old buildings and infrastructure in regular need of repair. The city spent time working with local merchants to find the best way to maintain the district. The result was a nonprofit with its own board and full-time executive director, funded in part by businesses and in part by the city. It guides maintenance and renovation, registers buildings for historic preservation and stages events – craft beer festivals, a farmer's market – to keep Uptown lively and support business.

This collaboration is given a structure by the Westerville Partnership. This kind of group is found in most Intelligent Communities in the US and Europe, made up of elected and administrative leaders of government, leaders of public and private education, and business executives devoted to the future of the community. The group meets quarterly to discuss the latest progress as well as new concerns and opportunities. Its members are in a position to make commitments to the group, launch action within their own organizations and maintain oversight and coordination.

Engagement is both a familiar idea to local governments and a completely new concept. It's familiar because municipalities work on engagement all the time: in meetings, newsletters and emails, surveys, press releases and social media posts.

But too much of that "engagement" is really marketing: selling policies and programs to the public after they have been decided and developed. What's new about engagement in the digital age is the opportunity to cheaply and easily bring constituents into the process of developing programs, facilities and infrastructure meant to benefit them.

Local governments can now engage in online brainstorming with a large number of citizens over an extended period of time without ever asking them to leave home. While policies are being worked out, governments can solicit input in stages to guide development, giving citizens and businesses the ability to propose action and see their suggestions incorporated into policies and plans. Ideas for digital services can be piloted at low cost and either scaled up or abandoned depending on results. Online incentive programs can attract volunteers and reward them for their work. Master plans can be modeled using digital animations to let people weigh in on the future shape of the place called home.

And there's an unexpected benefit to all this. Engagement ceases to be a separate process tacked on at the end of a project. It becomes a way of doing business. Talking to people, whether live or online, informs decisions from the earliest stages – and city staff has more time for engagement because digital tools reduce its cost in time and resources. "Educating the public" gradually gives way to a cooperative learning process for both the municipality and its people. Imaginative communities have even created open innovation programs, combining digital tools and live meetings, that solicit ideas for improving community life, conduct online voting to select worthy projects, provide seed funding to get them started, and publicize the results. Instead of marketing "products" that are already on the shelf, communities can tap the creativity and passion of constituents to power positive change from the start.

COMMUNITY PROFILE

Rossland, BC, Canada

Population: 3,500

This former mining town was voted "Canada's #1 Outdoor Town" by the outdoor magazine *Explore* for its stunning landscape and epic mountain trails. But it has not left its economy entirely in the hands of adventure-seeking tourists and skiers. Among its population of 3,500 are entrepreneurs who have also begun building an online business cluster. Prominent among these is ThoughtExchange, which has turned engagement into a business model. ThoughtExchange offers an online "crowdthinking" platform that helps groups of 5 to 50,000 share information, generate ideas and move toward decisions in a transparent process. Local governments, school district, colleges, credit unions and even UNESCO use it to engage stakeholders, energize their participation, and let them see their ideas contribute to positive change for the community or organization they care about. Based in Rossland, ThoughtExchange employs people located throughout British Columbia.

Connect

Engagement is the fuel in the tank, the sun on the solar cell, the wind in the turbine. The engagement of knowledgeable citizens and of organizations with a commitment to the community creates momentum that is hard to stop. That momentum drives the development of three new foundations of economic growth. The first is connectivity.

Broadband connectivity is the critical infrastructure of our century, just as electricity, railroads, highways and airplanes were over the previous hundred years. Broadband is defined in different ways in different places. All agree that is an "always on" service. It may be delivered over the airwaves, copper cables or optical fiber. Its speed can range from very slow – a megabit per second or less – to blindingly fast: a gigabit per second or more.

Whatever the speed, the power of broadband is simple enough to express. It creates a fast connection between your computer or mobile device and billions of devices and users around the world. It is a digital overlay to our physical world that is revolutionizing how we work, play, live, and educate, entertain and govern ourselves.

In most of the world, broadband is a private-sector business. That means it is subject to the rules of profit and loss, often interpreted by companies that hold a monopoly or near monopoly on service. The economics are simple: it is more profitable to serve a large number of customers located close together than a small number of customers spread far apart. You can earn a better return serving customers with lots of money than customers without. Investment flows to the former places and steers clear of the latter, except in cases where a local carrier is dedicated to delivering a higher quality of service to more customers than sheer economics dictates.

This reality creates the pattern visible in most of the industrialized world. Cities and prosperous suburbs have access to high-speed and reliable service and – where there is effective competition among providers – enjoy a competitive price. The exception is in neighborhoods judged too poor or difficult to serve to be financially attractive. As suburb gives way to exurb and rural lands, speed, reliability and price take a turn for the worse, leaving some locations with nothing but dial-up access or low-speed mobile phone service almost unusable for today's internet.

Taking Action

When communities decided to take action on broadband, they have a wide range of options. Most of the options have the same goal: to make the community a more attractive market for private-sector investment in digital connectivity. The most powerful way to do so is to *reduce the upfront investment required to serve the market, which lowers the risk and increases the profit potential.*

Local governments can also take steps to make the revenue case by demonstrating demand that may not be visible to private telcos. In one US county, the executive team worked with municipalities, school districts, water districts and other authorities to determine how much they were spending on telecommunications. It totaled US$50 million per year. That was big enough sum that the county was able to persuade a cable TV company to build a fiber network to serve these public-sector customers. It evolved over time into an 800-mile network serving 3,500 governments, agencies and businesses. But it all began with an effort to put the demand already in the marketplace to new use.

What are the Options?

Many leaders of local government are surprised to find that they *have* options. But they do. These range from steps that are not in the least controversial, because they call on the accepted authority of local government, to actions that put local government into competition with the private sector. *That's* controversial just about everywhere.

Broadly speaking, most communities have five options. They are not exclusive – rather, they are a set of steps on a staircase that leads upward to high-quality connectivity.

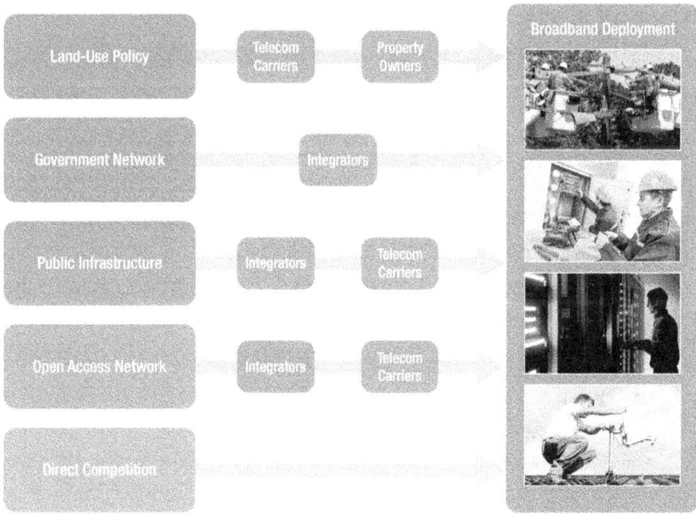

Land-use policy

Creative governments can direct the accepted tools of land-use policy to encourage broadband deployment, including:

- Mapping existing broadband networks to identify gaps, then bringing that knowledge to negotiations with private-sector carriers.
- Improving access policies and fees for poles and conduit.
- Requiring the installation of conduit during all street excavation for lease to carriers.
- Changing building codes to require that new and renovated developments be broadband-ready.

Separately and together, these actions make local markets less expensive and more attractive to new market entrants.

COMMUNITY PROFILE

Loma Linda, California, USA

Pop: 22,000 I Smart21 Community 2007

In Loma Linda, city government created a Connected Community project that envisioned every building connected with a 10 Gbps network. As part of implementation, it created what it called The Loma Linda Standard for all new residential and commercial construction as well as remodeling affecting more than 50% of a structure. The standard defined how internal cabling, the "wiring closet," the demarcation and external conduit networks were to be constructed to ensure that every resident or tenant of every building had the potential to access high-speed broadband services. The standard created a "bias toward broadband" among developers that proved transformative for the community. From 2004 to 2007, nearly a dozen projects went into development that used the Loma Linda Standard.

Government network

In most jurisdictions, governments can build and operate networks to serve their own facilities. This investment is easy to justify, because it replaces monthly telecom bills and typically pays off in less than five years. Using the network, government can deploy free Wi-Fi in public locations and develop online constituent services that increase user demand for broadband.

Public investment in networks also begins to change how incumbent private carriers view the costs and benefits of continuing to withhold investment in extending and upgrading their own networks.

COMMUNITY PROFILE

Regional Municipality of York, Ontario, Canada

Pop: 1,187,000 I Smart21 Community 2018

The Regional Municipality of York is a regional government body made up of 11 separate municipalities, ranging from suburban cities to rural townships. It delivers shared services – courts, police, public health and housing, to name a few – across all the communities, saving money and reducing geographic inequities.

In 2002, as an experiment, the York Region installed a one-kilometer fiber connection between two of its buildings. The experiment was a success: it was much cheaper than leasing connectivity from a provider and offered better control of network performance as a bonus.

Fast-forward to the present day and the Region operates a +200-kilometer fiber network connecting hundreds of municipal buildings, universities, schools and hospitals, as well as the telecom and data service companies that deliver service. The network carries internet and intranet services and data streams from digital monitoring systems, traffic management systems, cameras, and water and wastewater monitoring, as well as supporting public safety and social service operations.

By 2015, the growing operation was in need of a better operating model and, after study, the Region created a public corporation, YTN Telecom Network, and re-launched itself under the trade name YorkNet in 2018. The company developed a 10-year capital plan that is expanding the network three-fold, with special emphasis on pushing fiber into the many rural and underserved locations in the region.

Previous expansion has already had important impacts. A 30-kilometer link to a node on the national ORION research network made this 10 Gbps service available to researchers at a regional health center and university. The existence of the fiber network gave the York Region the ability to compete for a C$500 million federal fund supporting rural and remote broadband. A fiber swap deal with a private-sector provider motivated the company to push its service into a hard-to-reach rural community, and the continued expansion of the network is leading more providers to lease capacity and add revenue to the top line.

Creating public infrastructure

Building infrastructure is the traditional business of government. Some local governments build not just roads and sewers but "dark" telecommunications assets: conduit networks, optical fiber networks and wireless towers. They lease this infrastructure to carriers and organizations with major communications needs. Those buyers install equipment, activate circuits and deliver services.

Lease payments cover the capital, maintenance and upgrade costs of the network and contribute to the general fund. This approach creates greater competition in the market while steering clear of concerns about government competing with the private sector.

COMMUNITY PROFILE

Dublin, Ohio, USA

Pop: 41,000 I Top7 Intelligent Community 2011

Following telecommunications deregulation in 1996, Dublin began installing a network of underground conduit to encourage deployment of broadband by private carriers. A public-private partnership with the Fishel Company soon followed, and by 2003, Dublin had built the DubLink fiber network to connect city facilities and replace telephone company service. Dublin's contribution to the project came from tax-increment financing bonds, funded by future increases in tax revenue that would result from the improvements being financed.

In managing the network, the city drew a bright line between public and private use. The city delivers no services except for governmental use, and leases either conduit space or its own dark fiber to carriers serving the local market.

But as Dublin installed more and more fiber in its conduits, it began doing capacity-sharing deals with other organizations. DubLink now interconnects with Columbus FiberNet, which reaches the state capital and four other cities in the metro area. It partners with the Ohio Supercomputer Center (OSC), carrying some of the traffic on OSC's 1,600-mile fiber backbone. In return, the OSC and Dublin joined forces to create the Central Ohio Research Network, a fiber infrastructure connecting governments, schools and businesses to Ohio colleges, universities, research institutes and Federal labs. Other fiber transport partnerships include Central Ohio Broadband, linking with other cities that have developed fiber networks, and agreements with two carrier hotels in Columbus to exchange traffic in return for giving DubLink customers connection to global carriers.

Open access network

Some communities go beyond "dark" infrastructure to create open access networks. They build, activate and manage a government-owned or public-private network. It provides the "transport layer" – the foundation level of digital connection between physical locations. On this foundation, companies and carriers operate the services that meet the needs of their users. By further reducing the costs and risks for the private sector, open access networks have proven their ability in many different markets to produce a sharp increase in competition. The one location in which their effectiveness has been limited is in truly rural markets with population density so low that the costs of construction and operation are too high to make possible an attractive fee structure for carriers. But a mix of higher and lower density can overcome this limitation, as Parkland County shows.

COMMUNITY PROFILE

Parkland County, Alberta, Canada

Pop: 32,000 I Smart21 Community 2018

Parkland County is a county-sized municipality that has applied the open-access network model specifically to meet the needs of a rural region. Parkland County is prosperous. Its primary industries include power generation, forestry, coal, oil and gas, advanced manufacturing, transportation, logistics and agriculture. Most of this economic activity is concentrated in the east, within the economic zone of Edmonton, the provincial capital. The small cities, towns, villages and hamlets to the west, for all their natural beauty, lack employment opportunities and see a steady exodus of youth. One factor in the west's isolation is lack of access to broadband, with its potential to level the economic playing field.

In 2012, Parkland County completed the core of a network of 20 utility-grade communication towers, six of which have a fiber backhaul to the nearest Alberta SuperNet Point of Presence. Capitalized by grants, the towers have power and terrestrial connectivity and are open to operators of first-responder networks, mobile networks and wireless Internet Service Providers (WISPs), who need only rent space on a tower and install a radio to be in business. The towers are designed to allow multiple service providers to collocate on them as well, making it more affordable for companies to provide services in regions with low population density. Parkland County has rugged terrain and is heavily forested, so plans call for construction of an "in-fill" network of smaller towers to extend service to even more of the population. The business model produced breakeven on operating costs within four years, with the more popular towers in the east helping to subsidize the less popular ones in the west, and take-up by WISPs, integrators and government agencies has been strong.

Direct competition

The most extreme step communities can take is to compete directly with the private sector. This typically happens when private telephone and cable incumbents oppose all efforts at collaboration, most often in rural communities where not even the construction of dark or open access networks can make the market attractive to outside competitors.

One of the hidden advantages that many rural communities bring to this work is ownership of electric and water utilities – the legacy of previous waves of public investment in infrastructure that private companies were unwilling to fund. Having wires or pipes already connecting with every premise makes it far cheaper to add a telecom connection.

Regardless of how they are built, these networks have a mission very different from those of the private sector: to contribute to economic growth and better quality of life for residents, businesses and institutions.

COMMUNITY PROFILE

Bristol, Virginia, USA

Pop: 17,500 I Top7 Intelligent Community 2009

Like many rural American communities, Bristol Virginia owns and operates its own electric company, Bristol Virginia Utilities (BVU). In 1998, Bristol's city council voted to allow BVU to construct a fiber-optic backbone to improve communications and control among its eight electric substations. The business case was straightforward and the implementation successful. By 2000, BVU had extended the network to local schools and government offices, which reduced the city's operating costs and expanded the capabilities available to users. It also spurred demands from local businesses and real estate developers to provide service to them. So, in 2001, the council and BVU agreed to begin offering fiber-to-the-user (FTTU) service, branded OptiNet, to all residents and businesses.

Private-sector carriers were quick to challenge the move. One incumbent objected to the Virginia public utility commission, which regulates communications, stating that Virginia law barred municipalities from offering retail telecommunications services. Such a law was indeed on the books but, in Bristol's view, had been rendered invalid by passage of the Federal Telecommunications Act of 1996. Only after Bristol sued the state did the Virginia General Assembly pass legislation in 2002 overturning the old law. As BVU prepared its commercial launch later that year, the incumbent cable TV operator claimed that the utility lacked the legal authority to provide television service. A court agreed. BVU returned to the Assembly seeking legislative and charter changes, which were granted in 2003. But later that year, the telephone company's chief financial officer was back in the state capital testifying before a commission on the issue of cross-subsidies. The incumbent accused BVU of charging phone rates that were below its costs and making up the difference on other services. The commission ruled against the complaint. Finally, after three years and $2.5 million in legal fees, BVU had won the right to deliver retail communications.

As it turned out, the private sector was right to fear competition from BVU. Market research conducted by the company in 2001 suggested that 70% of respondents might switch telephone and television service from the incumbent operator, while half might switch internet service. By August 2008, BVU's OptiNet FTTU service had captured more than 62% of the available residential and business market in its service area, thanks to effective marketing to electric customers with whom BVU already had a relationship. Despite millions of dollars of investment, OptiNet reached financial self-sufficiency on $16 million in net revenues in the 2009 fiscal year. A 2008 study conducted for the BVU Board determined that OptiNet customers, while enjoying the bandwidth bonanza of FTTU, had saved nearly $10 million over incumbent competitors' rates since the start of service.

By then, the OptiNet service area was no longer limited by the city lines. BVU entered into partnership with the Cumberland Plateau Planning District Commission in 2003 to build CPC OptiNet. Managed by BVU, the network began with a 45-mile fiber-optic circuit reaching to Richlands, Virginia, funded by grants from the US government and the Virginia Tobacco Commission. It grew gradually to 200 miles across four rural counties with the help of additional grants. (The Tobacco Commission distributes money paid to the state by US tobacco companies following the 1998 settlement of the largest class-action lawsuit in US history.) BVU's success in designing, building and operating the network led it to establish a business unit called BVU FOCUS, which stands for Finding Opportunities for Communities. BVU FOCUS offers consulting and management services to other entities that seek to build advanced telecom networks. The unit's first customer in 2007 was MI-Connection, a telecom co-op owned by two communities in North Carolina. Under BVU's management, the $80 million network grew its customer base nearly 5% in its first year and exceeded budget by 27%.

Attracting or developing high-quality broadband isn't easy. To succeed, you need to begin the job – not with technology plans or requests for proposal – but with learning to *think* like a telecommunications company. It's all about generating revenue and reducing the risk of losses, and the strategy you adopt will depend on the degree to which private carriers have already invested, what they are investing in and what opportunities they may be missing. This chapter has outlined five fundamental strategies, and there are many more variations on these themes.

The Unexpected Secret of Success

There is one more important way in which it helps to think like a telco. In every place where they operate a local network, telcos build what are called central offices. There's a reason for that, which goes far beyond technology.

According to one of the most successful private investors in local and long-distance networks, the central office is the key to the success of a local network as both a business proposition and a driver of economic development.

Hunter Newby is a former telecom executive and now a venture investor in national, regional and local high-capacity networks. He believes that most municipalities seeking to build a network miss the most important factor in that network's success. It is the location of the central office: the network operations center where every element of the network joins and where other networks can connect to it. He recommends that communities think carefully about its location, because it can become the hub of economic development based on proximity to a high-capacity on-ramp to the network. More importantly, he recommends that communities do not just build the minimum "meet me" facility that connects networks. Instead, they should build a full-fledged data center.

Building your own data center, either 100% owned by the municipality or owned in partnership with a private company, delivers three big benefits.

- It supports the municipality's own network and data processing needs. What better place can there be for the city to manage its data operations, in terms of access and reliability, than from the center of the network?
- It offers high-quality collocation space for other networks. More than just a place to connect, a real data center provides infrastructure including uninterruptible power, high-capacity air-conditioning, cages for equipment, overhead cable trays and redundant, high-capacity data connections. The major providers of service, from national telecom operators to such content provider as Netflix, consider this kind of infrastructure essential for their local deployment.
- It creates potential for a new range of high-value services to local business. This can be the hosting of their applications on the data center's servers, which offer a level of reliability unavailable to most businesses on their own. Some communities have gone further: one city in Taiwan that is home to hundreds of small manufacturers licensed and hosted an enterprise resource planning (ERP) system for them that improved their productivity and – most importantly – opened up business opportunities for them with much larger companies. Needless to say, the municipal data center can deliver these services for less than private companies.

For most communities, the idea of developing a data center on top of a network may seem beyond reach. But it could be the decision that ensures the success of the entire project.

What is the Right Choice?

There is no one right choice for every community. Laws vary by jurisdiction and can sometimes make it difficult or impossible for a government to invest in communications infrastructure. One of the more infamous examples in the US is in the state of Louisiana. The city of Lafayette built a competitive network in 2009 to improve service to residents and businesses. Incumbent companies rose up and persuaded the state legislature to pass a bill forbidding any other municipality to do the same, in contravention of national law.

Residents can also be uncomfortable with the risks of large investment in communications infrastructure, which they are not accustomed to seeing on the municipality's balance sheet. Finally, there is the question of demand. Even relatively low-risk strategies will succeed only if a large enough percentage of residents feel strongly about the lack of adequate, competitively priced connectivity. That percentage can be a moving target: grassroots efforts in cities and counties can build support over time by making people aware that they do not have to accept the status quo. But without enough support, it is hard for any municipality to change its digital destiny.

The options are many and the choice is yours. If there is one thing to take away from this book, it is that you have choice. There is always something you can do, and every reason why the time to begin taking action is now.

Work

In 1973, the legendary management consultant Peter Drucker added a new phrase to the language. He forecast that, within two decades, it would become impossible to live in the American middle class by doing manual labor. It was a shocking prediction at the time. Before there were personal computers or supercomputers masquerading as phones in your pocket, Drucker foresaw that *knowledge* would become a major source of value in the economy. He called the new work that would be required to enter the middle class "knowledge work" and the people who performed it "knowledge workers."

Drucker's words were prophetic. In 2009, a report from the Organization of Economic Cooperation and Development, found that half of the long-term unemployed in the world's 30 richest nations – those being hammered by the Great Recession – were young people who left school at the minimum legal age.[7] A 2018 study from the US Bureau of Labor Statistics found that the average weekly earnings of a high school graduate were only $712, compared with $1,173 for the owner of a bachelor's degree and $1,836 for someone with an engineering, law or other professional degree. Multiply that by 10 years and the bachelor's degree holder would take home $240,000 more than the high school graduate, while the professional would walk away with an additional $584,000. [8]

Today, all desirable jobs in industrialized economies – and increasingly in developing economies as well – require a higher component of knowledge than they did in the past, whether the work takes place in an office, a factory, a construction site or a retail store. It is by applying knowledge and specialized skills that employees add enough value to what they do to justify the cost of employing them – compared to the alternative of automating away their function. That has made a continuous improvement in an expanding range of skills the only route to personal prosperity.

This unforgiving new condition places an awful burden on people who lack ready access to quality education – principally the poor and minorities – and lack as well the support of educated parents and all the enrichment activities that affluence provides. But there is no escaping it. More than three decades ago, in 1983, upper income households in the United States owned about 60% of total US wealth. Thanks to the high returns from education, they increased their share to 79% by 2016. Meanwhile, the share of total wealth owned by middle income and lower income households *dropped by half,* to 17% and 4% respectively.[9] The US is an extremely unequal country compared to other rich nations, but the same pattern is visible everywhere.

Building a Ladder of Opportunity

What can the leaders of a city, a county or region do to put their people on the right side of this global trend?

The first step is the same as you would take for a hurricane, flood or infectious disease. It is to recognize that trouble is knocking on your door and demanding action. Sure, forces beyond your control are at work – but that does not excuse you from lacing up your boots and getting to work for the good of your community.

The second step is to begin a patient, persistent transformation in how your community delivers education to children and adults. You are now in the business of building a knowledge workforce, and that takes, believe it or not, a ladder.

Public education, work-study and apprenticeships, colleges and universities are thought of as rungs on an educational ladder that prepares children for life as working adults. But in most places, that ladder is far less sturdy than it appears. There is a curriculum in the public schools that advances students, year after year, in skills and understanding. Those schools operate in their own silos, however, with little interaction by faculty and students across elementary, pre-secondary and secondary grades. There is even less interaction with key employment sectors, from private business to nonprofits, even though the local economy would benefit by alerting students to career opportunity.

Where communities are home to trade schools, two-year colleges and four-year universities, these too often operate in their own silos, separate from each other and with no notion of the skill requirements of employers in the region.

Intelligent Communities push against this tradition by creating genuine collaboration among local government, educators and employers. The goal is to produce a knowledge-rich workforce that is in rough balance with the region's demand for labor, and to help individuals and employers continuously improve their knowledge and skills to strengthen their competitive advantage.

And to say it one more time: "knowledge workers" are found not just in white-collar settings but on the factory floor, the warehouse, the restaurant and the farm. The barista at the coffee shop needs to keep the Wi-Fi running and the warehouse clerk uses digital equipment to manage inventory. As the title of a report from the Province of Ontario, Canada put it a few years ago, "menial is menial no more."

The diagram on the next page illustrates the connections that can build a ladder of opportunity for the next generation and make tomorrow more prosperous than today.

Building a Knowledge Workforce at a Glance:

- Local, regional and state/provincial **governments** act as conveners, bringing together educational leaders through commissions, advisory boards and other structures that create a permanent platform for collaboration.
- Secondary schools send students and programs into **elementary schools** to make an early introduction to content on future local careers.
- Universities and colleges interconnect with **secondary schools** to provide students with advanced learning opportunities.
- **Universities** interconnect with career-focused **colleges** to share research programs and career courses, and provide college students with access to 4-year degrees
- **Employers** bring real-world career content, business mentors, work-study programs, internship and other programs into education to expand students' awareness of their local career opportunities and create excitement.
- Individual **citizens, civic groups** and **businesses** and **institutions** provide demand for programs that enrich education and support them through fundraising and volunteer leadership.

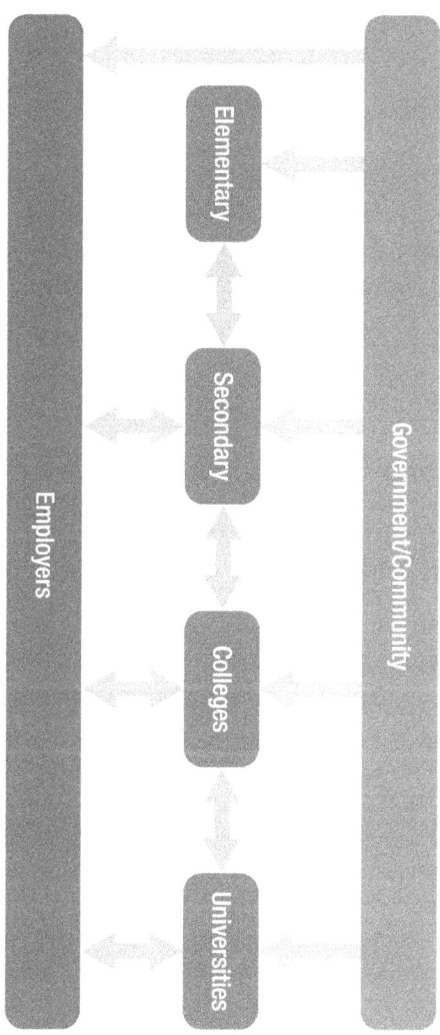

As they tackle this work, big and small communities face different challenges. Large communities have the advantage of scale and the disadvantage of being big, complex and cumbersome. Progress at changing something as politically sensitive as education can be glacial. Small communities lack resources, but their work can often be jump-started by a few people sharing a passion for positive change.

COMMUNITY PROFILE

Winnipeg, Manitoba, Canada

Pop: 812,000 I Top7 Intelligent Community 2018

Winnipeg is a midsize city that stands alone on the plains of Manitoba. It is a good place to see the ladders of opportunity at work. In a central place on that ladder is Sisler High School. Located in a low-income neighborhood, it used to be one of the worst-performing schools in the city. It is now one of the best.

The singular focus at Sisler is on ensuring their students are ready for the next step after high school. It teaches the full secondary curriculum with extensive arts, music and drama offerings. But it began focusing seriously on technology years ago with the ambitious goal, in the words of their principal, "to utterly transform pedagogy."

The high school has long-standing partnerships with the University of Winnipeg and University of Manitoba. At Sisler, students can finish their first year of university by the end of grade 12, which requires the school to offer five university-accredited courses. To supplement these courses, Sisler also partners with the universities and Red River College to give its seniors access to post-secondary programs at those institutions.

Sisler also sends students to visit elementary grades and conduct digital media workshops – a recent digital media competition for 4th graders was run by Sisler and judged by a senior executive of a major gaming company, Electronic Arts.

A partnership with the Vancouver Film School (VFS) brings the film school's instructors into Sisler digital media classes through live-streaming sessions and in-person workshops. Live streaming is a technology that Sisler students and teachers taught VSF, and it has enabled that college to deliver instruction to students in 40 nations.

Partnerships with the filmmaker DreamWorks Pictures and effects studio Industrial Light & Magic have connected Winnipeg students with their executives. Medical centers in the city provide live streaming of surgery, and students in environmental science classes interact online with activists in Africa. School officials estimate they have connected more than 30,000 students to such real-life content.

The standout program at the high school is cybersecurity. Teachers and parents raised a half million Canadian dollars to create a virtual enterprise network on which students learn basic and advanced cybersecurity management, from protecting individual computers to safeguarding a corporate-level network. The school has competed in an annual CyberPatriot competition hosted by the US Air Force Association, attended by generals and senior officials of the CIA and NSA. For three years in a row, the Sisler team brought home the top prize out of 3,500 teams, and many of its students have been hired right out of high school.

The Power to Convene

For municipal leaders, the idea of influencing primary, secondary and higher education may seem foreign territory. In most places, national governments set standards and establish curricula. Even nations that favor local control, like the United States, have state or provincial authorities telling school districts how to teach. And when it comes to community colleges, technical schools and universities, why should they listen to the Mayor or members of Council about educational priorities?

But in much of the world, educators know they are struggling to give students an education relevant to the world they will enter as adults. The success of world-famous companies that got their start at universities has also changed how nearly every college looks at entrepreneurship. The chances of finding individual educators, public school principals and college presidents open to innovation are better than they have ever been.

Local government leaders have a unique and undervalued ability: the power to *convene*. They can get leaders in education, business and institutions to attend meetings and encourage them to share problems and develop solutions together. For one city, the solution may be creating a seamless path for community college students to finish their education at a university. For another, it may be work-study or apprenticeship programs designed in collaboration with businesses. For a third, it may be hiring university students to help at-risk high-school kids pursue projects that spark their interest and keep them in school.

Developing the first successful project is hard. It takes patience, flexibility and deal-making skills. But that first successful project is a catalyst for the next and the next – until, over time, adding new rungs to the ladder of opportunity becomes a habit, business as usual, just the way things are done. What seemed outlandish at one time can create a lasting legacy that benefits the people of today and tomorrow.

Innovate

Innovation means creating something new, developing a new process or finding a new source of supply. It is what drives growth in the economy – and we have a Nobel Prize winner to thank for proving it. In 1987, economist Robert Solow won the prize for demonstrating that introducing and using new technology was responsible for as much as 80% of the growth in the national economy.

That number puts the issue in stark perspective. Would you prefer to have the place you live participate in the 80% of growth coming from innovation, or are you content with the 20% that comes from doing the same old thing? In almost every place called home, people would prefer Choice #1.

But how does a city, town or region get into the innovation game? The first step is to make it a leadership priority. Believe it or not, every community of every size needs an innovation strategy today. Like much else in the ICF Method, that can seem a little crazy to people who were elected to make housing more affordable, improve access to recreation or keep taxes under control. But it is the imperative of the digital age.

Fortunately, innovation is not the same thing as invention. In Dr. Solow's formulation, growth comes as much from putting new technology to use as it does to creating it. Perhaps more. Back in 2009, a post by an anonymous Wikipedia user noted that "Invention is the conversion of cash into new ideas. Innovation is the conversion of new ideas into cash." For most local economies, the second sentence is where the action is.

Once they accept the innovation challenge, Intelligent Communities approach it in two ways. They work to create an ecosystem that promotes innovation in the private sector, while also innovating in how government does its job.

Private-Sector Innovation

That word "ecosystem" needs a moment's explanation. In nature, it describes the interaction of plants, animals, land and weather that sustains life, each supporting the others in a balance arrived at over millennia. An innovation ecosystem also arises from interactions among many players, whose work supports each other and creates self-sustaining momentum.

The innovation ecosystem of an Intelligent Community draws on educational institutions, established businesses and ambitious individuals with a passion for making somcthing new. To turn those assets into self-sustaining progress, local government works with businesses and institutions to create a structure of programs and facilities that encourage and challenge talented people to innovate.

Private-Sector Innovation at a Glance:

- **Local government** acts as a convener and seed-funding partner of educators, businesses and citizens intent on improving the economic prospects of the community.
- An **educational sector**, an established **business sector** and engaged **citizens** bring knowledge, resources and ambition to the effort.
- Collaborative development and investment by them in:
    - Public **hackathons**, **apps contests** and other STEM events.

- **Makerspaces** where anyone can bring an idea and make it real (and potentially profitable) with the informal support of other innovators.
- **Incubators** where potential entrepreneurs go through a disciplined process to turn concepts into saleable products and services, then find their initial customers.
- **Accelerators** that take the survivors of incubation and help them mature into sustainable enterprises with growth potential.
- **Innovation Districts** that house these facilities as well as R&D centers, open innovation labs and space for established and new businesses, including offices, co-working spaces, manufacturing facilities and wet labs.

- **Product and service innovation by established businesses**, working with the educational sector, often as part of public-private innovation programs.
- **Start-ups**, which emerge from makerspaces, incubators and accelerators.
- Successful start-ups attract **risk capital** from angels, grants, venture funds and private equity that permit them to scale the business significantly.
- Successful entrepreneurs and growing established businesses tend to **reinvest** in the innovation ecosystem from which they benefited. It is succeeding generations of innovators, each giving back, who ultimately drive the community forward.

You may expect to find programs and structure like these in a big city where technology companies dominate. But they can be found in midsize and small cities around the world, operating at a scale appropriate to their population to create a multi-faced innovation ecosystem that generates growth.

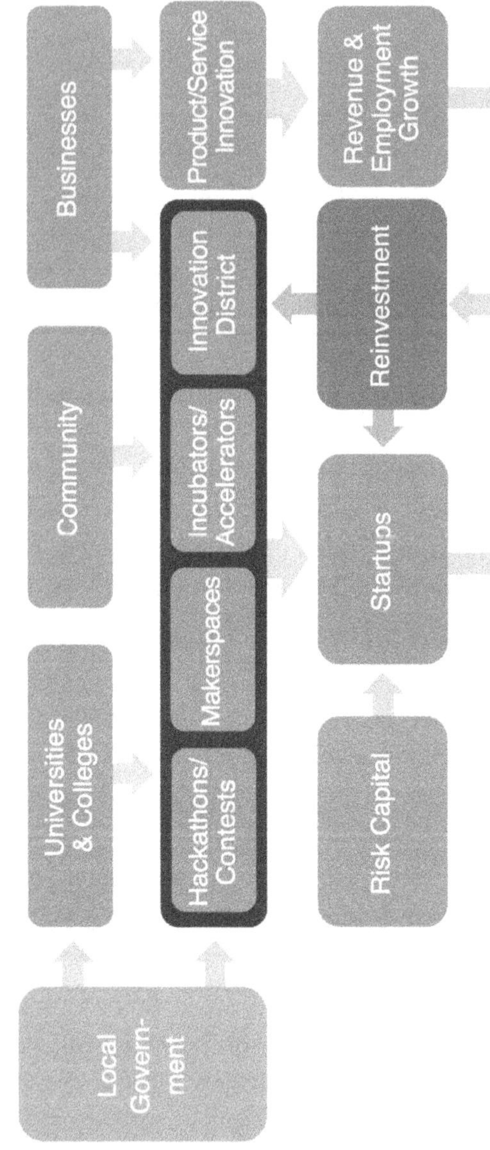
Local Govern-ment
Universities & Colleges
Community
Businesses
Hackathons/ Contests
Makerspaces
Incubators/ Accelerators
Innovation District
Product/Service Innovation
Risk Capital
Startups
Reinvestment
Revenue & Employment Growth
© 2019 Intelligent Community Forum

COMMUNITY PROFILE

Eindhoven, Netherlands

Pop: 216,000 I Intelligent Community of the Year 2011

Eindhoven is a very successful place. A midsize city, it is the center of a region that absorbs 36% of all private Dutch R&D spending, produces one-quarter of all Dutch exports and is home to globally recognized companies from Phillips to ASML. Eighteen percent of all Dutch automotive jobs are in Eindhoven, and nine percent of all life technology employment. The Eindhoven University of Technology, with more than 7,000 students, is considered one of the top three research universities in Europe.

But Eindhoven is also a manufacturing center in a high-cost country. By focusing on producing high-value, technology-based products, it is in competition with fast-growing manufacturing centers in nations with much lower costs. It is also saddled with Europe's demographics, in which a low birth rate and aging population is reducing the regional labor force.

Eindhoven's answer to these challenges is a public-private partnership called Brainport Development (www.brainport.nl). It was born in crisis, at a time when Phillips – which founded the city – moved its headquarters and much of its operations to Amsterdam, eliminating tens of thousands of jobs. Led by Eindhoven, the cities of the region formed and funded Brainport as a membership organization of employers, universities, institutes and the chamber of commerce.

The Brainport method brings together the players from business, government, institutions and citizen groups. A small professional staff meets regularly with stakeholders to identify opportunities and develop projects that draw on the skills and resources of partner organizations. Then it manages the projects carefully until they produce results and gain the ability to become self-sustaining.

The range of Brainport projects is extraordinarily wide. The Automotive Technology Center involves 125 organizations in collaborative projects that, from 2005 to 2008, generated €4.5m in new investment. The start-up of new high-tech systems and ICT companies is stimulated by incubators with names like Catalyst, Beta II and the Device Process Building.

Design Connection Brainport manages a wide range of projects in design and technology, to encourage the industrial design expertise that is essential to all industrial clusters.

The most long-standing innovation projects of Brainport concern broadband. From 1999 to 2005, the Dutch government funded a pilot program called Kenniswijk ("Knowledge City") to subsidize installation of fiber to the home. The program ended after connecting 15,000 homes, but it was followed by a classic Brainport project: Be-linked, which brought together companies, institutions, social organizations, governments and residents to promote broadband deployment and applications. Over the ensuing years, it has stimulated a remarkable range of activity.

Digital technologies are also brought to bear on creating a quality of life that attracts and retains the digitally literate. Digital City Eindhoven attracts a half-million visitors monthly to a Web-based social media tool that encourages residents to learn more about the region. A WMO Portal involves 20 organizations in answering resident questions on health care, social services and housing. Bestuuronline puts political meetings in the city of Eindhoven online, while Virtual Helmond involves residents of that city in decision-making about planning, building designs and street furniture.

An online game called SenseOfTheCity allows anyone with a GPS-equipped mobile phone to create a personal map of the city and identify what they like best and least. A 12-day festival called STRP, which attracts 225,000 visitors, features music, film, live performances, interactive art, light art and robotics. GLOW is another festival that celebrates Eindhoven's history as home to the Phillips lighting division. The center of the city of Eindhoven is transformed for 10 days into an open-air museum of design in light, much of it interactive, for 65,000 visitors.

Public-Sector Innovation

Innovation is not just a game for business to play. Intelligent Communities pursue innovation in government services and processes to reduce operating costs, improve service delivery and make governing more transparent to the public. This is where the Intelligent Community meets the Smart City to generate gains that save taxpayers money, reduce costs, eliminate waste and improve services to constituents.

Public Sector Innovation at a Glance:

- **Government** leads by example, making innovations in government services and processes that make a meaningful contribution to quality of life.
- Government collaboratively engages **citizens**, **businesses** and the **nonprofit sector** in helping to decide where innovation is most needed.
- Government turns to the **local technology sector** for practical advice on what is possible and likely to be most cost-effective.
- A resulting **Innovation Strategy** addresses real needs, sets ambitious goals and defines a realistic roadmap for accomplishing them.
- **IT projects** deliver on goals while creating demand for local technology companies' products and services.
- **Promotion** of successful projects drives adoption and demonstrate the innovation potential of the community.

When these projects deliver on their goals – providing real value to the citizens, businesses and nonprofits who helped to conceive them – they send strong signals to potential investors that the community is an ideal place to pursuit their goals.

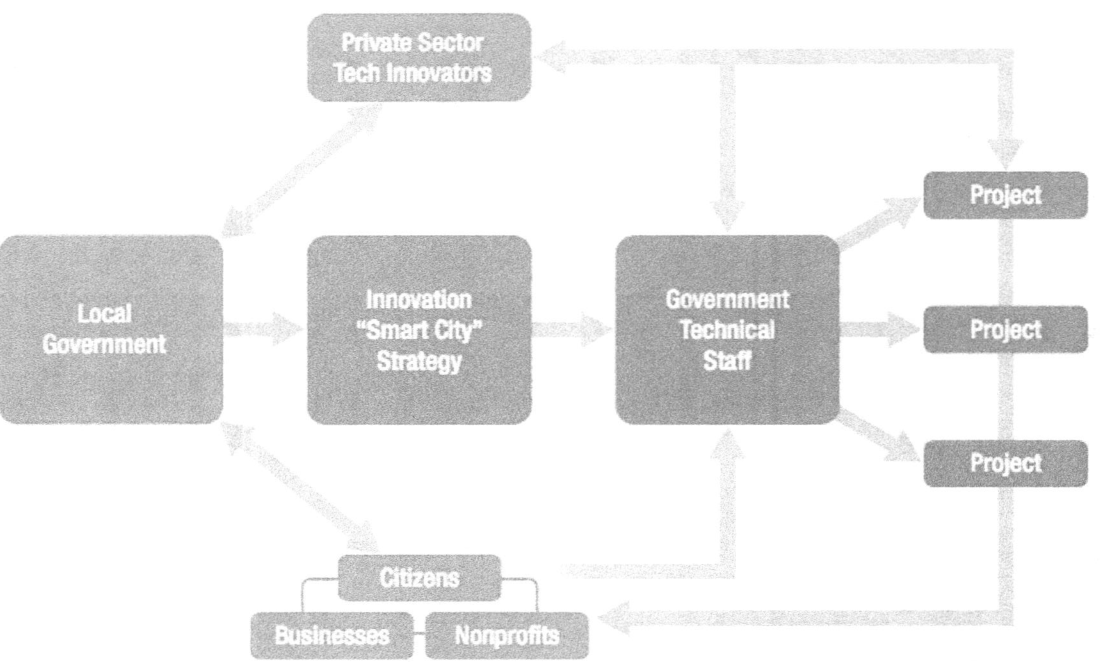
Private Sector Tech Innovators
Local Government
Innovation "Smart City" Strategy
Government Technical Staff
Project
Project
Project
Citizens
Businesses
Nonprofits

COMMUNITY PROFILE

Chiayi City, Taiwan

Pop: 269,000 I Top7 Intelligent Community 2018

Chiayi is small city by Taiwanese standard and is located in the south-central part of the island, remote from the massive industrial parks farther north. Ninety-five percent of its economy is in the low-tech services sector – wholesale and retail, transportation and warehousing, and accommodation and food – which employs three-quarters of the workforce.

In 2014, Chiayi was ranked as having the worst air quality in Taiwan, and Mayor Twu Shiing-jer, a physician, decide to dedicate his administration to improving life in the city in this and many other areas.

Working with the tech company ASUS, the city established a network of cloud-connected air-quality monitoring stations called Air Boxes. The results of measurement are displayed in real time on LED billboards on main access roads. A public electric bike network, with 58 charging stations, is reducing automobile trips, while an environmental education program is reaching schools and community groups. In 2015, the city reduced fine air particulate concentration by 12%, which represented the biggest gain in the nation.

The same year, Chiayi City established the "Solar Photovoltaic Setup and Promotion Team" and the "Renewable Energy Committee." The city's location on the Tropic of Cancer makes it an ideal place for solar energy development, and the city has currently installed solar panels on the rooftops of 70 public buildings. The buildings are capable of producing 3.6 megawatts of power annually and are expected to earn Chiayi NDT 77 million over the next 20 years.

Chiayi government and private carriers have blanketed the city with 1,000 Wi-Fi hotspots, ranking second for density in the nation. Over an 18-month period, more than 1.5 million users accessed the network. To support adoption, it created a government-citizen committee to hold public hearings, seminars, online idea generation and voting on priorities and projects. At the urging of that committee, Chiayi also completed an open data platform in 2016 and an E-Service Counter that provides single sign-on to more than 500 applications used by 210,000 subscribers.

To further spread E-Service access throughout the city, the Chiayi Transportation and Tourism Department is currently introducing intelligent bus stops with Wi-Fi available on their buses. The city has also equipped its 59 neighborhood directors with tablet PCs connected to the city's open data platform and E-Service applications, allowing them to function as mobile service stations for their neighborhoods. These directors help residents with information inquiries, online application usage and city surveillance reporting, among other services.

Health technology is the city's future, in the eyes of Mayor Twu. His administration is creating a Community Home Medical Care and Palliative Care Network to address Taiwan's aging population. There are now four hospitals and 33 clinics within the network, which aims to provide comprehensive care to the aged at home through a Smart Health Cloud Platform that already links in-home diagnostic equipment by 4G mobile to medical centers.

Connectivity, knowledge work and innovation are the engines of local economic growth in the digital age. When flows of data, investment, new services and products produce most of the world's prosperity, no place can afford to ignore their importance – and nearly every place has a chance to grab its share. Sitting on top of natural resources still has value, but not if it locks the community into cycles of boom and bust. Location still matters, but it is no longer destiny. What matters are the skills, dreams and ambitions of your people, how they work together to create growth, and the digital infrastructure that supports them.

But growth is only the starting point. It is the necessary foundation for a thriving community. To truly thrive, however, communities must look after *all* their people, not just the "digital natives." They must never stop thinking of ways to engage people in governing and to attract them with social and cultural riches. They must protect and improve the quality of life and resilience of the place called home, because it is a critical advantage in a fast-changing world.

Caring for the Community

Prosperity goes only so far. We can be affluent yet unmoored, outwardly successful but lacking the human connections that give life its meaning.

The life of a city begins with its people. Their satisfaction and happiness in that place depend on more than infrastructure, services and a paycheck. Given half a chance, people will make almost any place a home. We are deeply attracted to the familiar. We treasure comforting habits and known personalities. If that home rewards us with a great quality of life, however, the bond becomes so much deeper.

People need to care about the community, whether it is their town or village, their neighborhood or a single city block. They also need, just as much, to feel that the community cares for them in return. Caring for the community through times of great change is part of the project every Intelligent Community takes on.

It begins with the engagement efforts that make a city's people and organizations into its greatest champions. (See page 29.) It continues through efforts to include everyone in the community's future and tie the things that people love most about the community to its economic and social success. These efforts contribute to making the community a place that no resident wants to leave and new residents are eager to join.

Include

Even with a state-of-the-art network available to most homes and businesses, part of the population always remains offline. And being offline today carries real penalties, from lack of access to discount prices on shopping to the ability to do schoolwork or apply for a job. Those penalties tend to fall on people who are already on the margins of the economy and society, whether due to poverty, lack of education, racial or religious prejudice, age or disability. Their situation is made all the harder by the economic disruption wrought by the digital age on industries from manufacturing to retailing. The job opportunities that match their skills are declining, and they don't have what it takes to change with the times.

Intelligent Communities take care of the community by promoting *digital inclusion*: the principle that everyone in the community deserves to have access to the digital world and the skills to take advantage of it.

Why do they put time and resources into this problem? First of all, because it is the moral thing to do. But there are practical reasons as well. People who are excluded from the economy and society cost enormous amounts of money for social services, criminal justice and acute healthcare. They damage the social welfare of the whole community. The more people we include in the community's digital future, however, the better that future will be for everyone.

Digital exclusion affects more than people. Small-to-midsize enterprises (SMEs) are collectively the biggest employers in every community. Startup companies aside, they are also less likely to put digital technologies to work than bigger companies, because they are worried about costs, complexity and lack of support.

Eighty-nine percent of big companies in North America have plans to adopt or have already adopted a "digital-first" business strategy, according to a 2018 report from IDG.[10] Meanwhile, in 2017, 45% of small businesses did not even have a website and only 36% used theirs to communicate news to customers and potential customer, according to a CNBC/SurveyMonkey survey.[11] Because SMEs are so important to the local economy, Intelligent Communities include their owners in digital inclusion programs.

Employers require a different set of programs, though with a common focus on access, skills and motivation. One proven technique is to ask businesses to complete simple checklists that measure their digital readiness. The checklist leads to a readiness score for that organization with a comparison to other local companies and recommendations for improving it. The checklist process provides both specific help and peer pressure that can spur positive action. Employers scoring low for digital readiness can be targeted for training in digital skills and specific applications, typically provided by the local community or technical college. Many Intelligent Communities also create technology demonstration centers, where businesses can see and experiment with the latest technology before taking the plunge.

Digital inclusion at a Glance:

- **Identifies populations** most in need of intervention, as well as employers that are missing the opportunities of going digital.
- Provides **access** to broadband and information tech and **equips individuals and organizations with the ability to use them**.

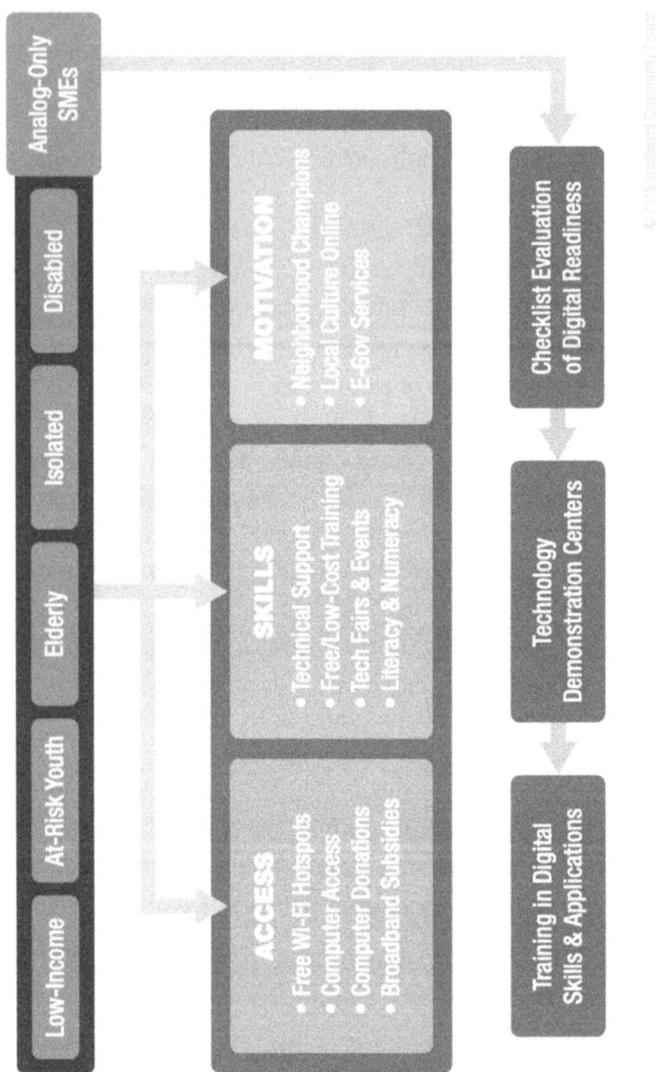

- Brings **technology and skills training** to meeting places: libraries, community centers and retirement homes.

- Involves library staff, students or the staff of local colleges and universities in spreading digital literacy.
- Creates programs that give people and organizations motivation to adopt technology and use it to improve their lives. This helps create an **attitude** of acceptance that enables communities to benefit from digital innovations.
- Engages employers in a focus on digital business improvement, such as through:
    - **Digital readiness checklists**, where employers can score themselves on their tech skills and infrastructure, compare themselves to their peers, and then seek help from local government and nonprofits.
    - **Technology demonstration centers**, where businesses can experiment with technology before beginning to invest in it.

COMMUNITY PROFILE

Knowle West, Bristol, United Kingdom

Pop: 12,000 I Smart21 Community 2017

Bristol is the largest city in the southwest of England, with a population of about a half million. It has a modern economy built on the creative media, electronics and aerospace industries, and its city-center docks have been redeveloped as centers of heritage and culture.

Yet even such vibrant midsize cities have pockets of deprivation, where poverty, poor education and the social ills that go with them are handed down from one generation to the next. For Bristol, that pocket is the neighborhood of Knowle West. The closure of a major factory in the Nineties caused large-scale job losses and a third of residents today are classified as economically inactive.

To give the 12,000 residents of Knowle West a chance at a better future, Bristol's Council has invested in digital-age programs that aim to transform life at the individual, family and community levels. Basic infrastructure is part of the mix. Bristol has developed the Filwood Green Business Park in Knowle West, which provides 76 units of "green" office and workshop space for small to midsized businesses, as well as shared office space for solo workers. It has expanded bus routes to better connect the neighborhood with the rest of Bristol, after surveys found that most residents needed to own a car to get to work.

Digital investment of another kind has created the Knowle West Media Centre, where residents receive free skills development programs including digital manufacturing and business basics. A work-study program trains residents while employing them on social action projects that give them work experience. After-school groups for children and young people teach digital literacy and creative skills, and supply leadership coaching for 18-25 year olds.

In the Junior Digital Producer program, young people who have been unemployed learn in-demand industry skills while delivering a community-based project. The Media Centre also has its own creative agency, Eight, where budding freelancers undertake paid commissions with the support of more experienced creatives. In its most recent year, users of the Media Centre produced nearly 500 pieces of furniture for the Filwood Green Business Park and created 8 businesses and community enterprises. Nearly 90% of participants in the Digital Producer program go onto paid work or self-employment.

Sustain

Quality of life has been defined as everything that makes a place worth calling home. Many things contribute to it: jobs and education, medical care and housing, recreation and culture, public safety, the relative cost of living and the natural or human-constructed beauty of the place. But one factor stands out, even if it tends to be taken for granted. Clean water and breathable air. Soils free of pollutants and poisons. And, increasingly, the resilience to withstand the subtle but powerful impact of climate change, in the form of freakish storms, flooding, drought, deadly heat waves and dangerous new diseases borne from the breakdown of ecosystems.

At the local level, a commitment to sustainability brings three benefits to an Intelligent Community.

First, sustainability is about improving local quality of life, from cleaner air and water to greener transportation and greater livability. High quality of live is a competitive advantage that help communities attract and retain both people and employers.

Second, it is a cause that all residents value and many feel passionately about. When sustainability projects genuinely involve local residents and organizations, they become powerful drivers of community engagement and pride. Once engaged, that passion can be harnessed for many other kinds of positive change.

Finally, sustainability has an economic dimension. It has become a growth industry around the world. Renewable energy capacity attracted US$2.6 trillion in investment from 2009 to 2019, which vaulted total capacity by a factor of four.[12] The global market for environmental remediation technologies, worth US$68 billion in 2017, is forecast to reach $83 billion by 2022.[13] Those numbers suggest that an economic development strategy that includes sustainability industries is a good bet for most communities.

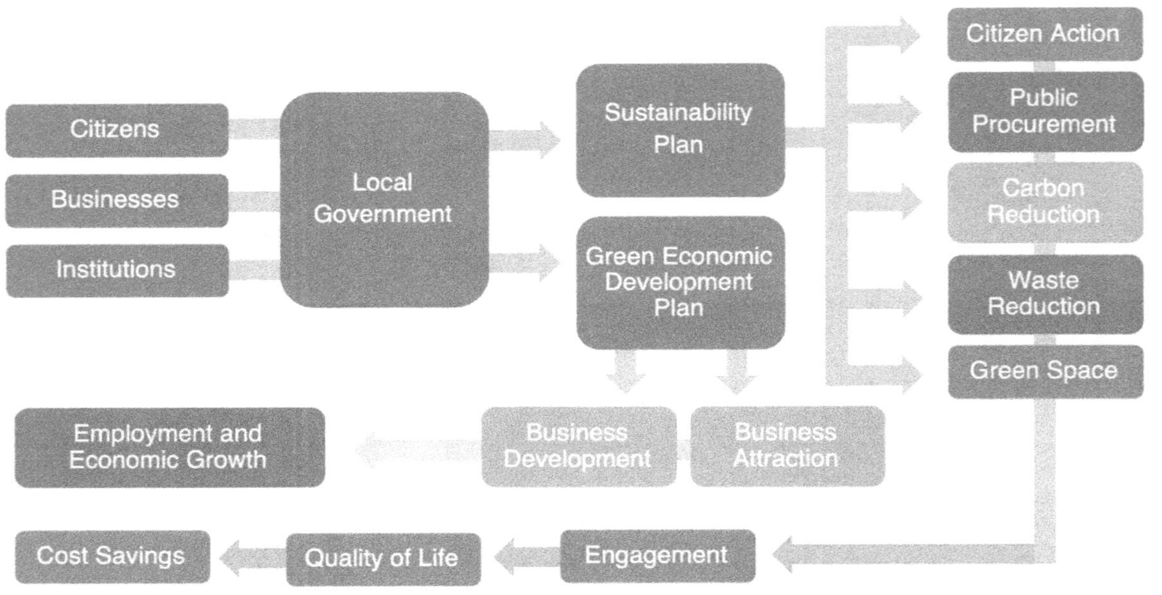
Citizens
Businesses
Institutions
Local Government
Sustainability Plan
Green Economic Development Plan
Citizen Action
Public Procurement
Carbon Reduction
Waste Reduction
Green Space
Employment and Economic Growth
Business Development
Business Attraction
Cost Savings
Quality of Life
Engagement
© 2020 Intelligent Community Forum

Sustainability at a Glance:

- **Local government** engaging with **citizens**, **businesses** and **institutions** to learn their concerns and collaborate in setting priorities. The issues are environmental – but also about quality of life, property values, government budgets and the cost of living and doing business in the community.
- Developing a **Sustainability Plan** that sets goals and identifies specific actions. These range from citizen action groups to changes in public procurement and land-use, and from waste reduction and recycling to energy conservation. They address water quality, air quality, alternative energy, and the resilience of the community to climate change. A range of Smart technologies are employed to find solutions, including cameras, drones and sensors.
- Focusing the innovation strategy and economic development programs on **green industries**, with the aim of growing any existing firms, producing new startups and attracting green businesses
- **Engaging citizens and groups** in carrying out the plan to save money, lower emissions, reduce consumption and improve quality of life.
- **Maintaining engagement and public support** through regular reporting on green industry development and sustainability measures.

COMMUNITY PROFILE

Sarnia-Lambton, Ontario, Canada

Pop: 127,000 I Top7 Intelligent Community 2019

Sarnia is the largest city in Lambton County, which extends from the shores of Lake Huron in the north to the Lake St. Clair in the south. Nearly 60% of the county's population is concentrated there, with the remaining 40% distributed across 2,800 square kilometers (695 sq mi) of the rest of the county. The sparsely populated county was, however, the site of North America's first commercially drilled oil well. Petrochemical and refining industries are still its largest manufacturing and employment sector, and Sarnia-Lambton considers itself the center of the Great Lakes Industrial Corridor. The other mainstays of the economy are agriculture and tourism

Farmers in the Cellulosic Sugar Producers Cooperative have worked with federal and provincial agencies, a local university and private-sector companies to research opportunities and develop a business plan for converting agricultural waste into cellulosic sugars. There is a ready market for these sugars in making multiple products. In 2016, the Cooperative announced that it would partner with Comet Biorefining to build a commercial-scale plant at the TransAlta Energy Park in Sarnia-Lambton. The completed plant is designed to produce 27 million kilograms of dextrose sugar syrup per year from corn stalks and wheat straw, and the Cooperative has signed agreements with a buyer to use the product in producing personal care products, plasticizers and polymers.

Alongside agricultural innovation, Sarnia-Lambton is focusing on renewable energy sources with the goal of eventually moving away from fossil-fuel-based feedstock. The county launched two initiatives to further this goal.

The Sarnia-Lambton Bio-Hybrid & Chemistry Cluster has attracted a number of bio-hybrid chemical companies to begin developing and testing their technologies in the county, leveraging Sarnia-Lambton's prosperous soybean, wheat and sugar beet farms as ideal sources of crop and bio-mass raw materials for new bio-chemical technologies. The cluster has also worked with Lambton's increasingly digital farming sector to supplant crude oil and petrochemical feedstocks. To provide state-of-the-art facilities for research in the area, Lambton College established a Center of Excellence in Energy & Bio-

Industrial Technologies in 2015 and added a $12m expansion to those facilities in 2016.

The Sarnia-Lambton Sustainable Energy Cluster scored its first major success when Sarnia-Lambton became home to one of the largest solar projects in North America, the Enbridge/First Solar 80 MW solar farm in 2014. The county has also attracted two large wind energy projects: Suncor Energy's Cedar Point Wind Power Project and NextEra Energy's Jericho Energy Centre. To further facilitate energy research, the county established the Lambton Energy Research Centre in 2016 as part of Lambton College's Applied Research & Innovation umbrella. LERC is an R&D center that supports energy-focused SMEs with their technology development, validation and commercialization.

COMMUNITY PROFILE

Melbourne, Victoria, Australia

Pop: 130,000 I Intelligent Community of the Year 2017

Melbourne, capital of the state of Victoria, is Australia's second largest municipality. A leading financial center, this city of 130,000 is the hub of a metropolitan area of 4.5 million people and home to the Australian film and television industries. In 2016, *The Economist* named Melbourne the world's most livable city for the sixth year in a row.

Melbourne makes sustainability strategy a community affair. Its Smart Blocks Solar Rebate program helps apartment owners and building managers install solar panels to reduce energy costs. The installation of a solar system on common property requires the owner or executive committee to work with tenants to develop the concept, build a business case, and engage apartment managers and suppliers. The Smart Blocks program provides advice throughout the process. It had installed 144 KW of solar through the end of 2015, saving apartment owners an average of A$25,000 on energy per year.

Melbourne's top score for livability is partly the product of a community plan called Future Melbourne. In 2016, the city began to refresh the plan, renaming it Future Melbourne 2026, through meetings of a Citizen's Jury made up of residents, workers and business executives. To broaden participation, it created a digital forum called Participate Melbourne, which lets members of the community contribute to decisions shaping the city's future.

The result has been 970 ideas for projects and a program of events that engaged participation from 2,000 people. Meanwhile, the 250,000 registered users of Participate Melbourne logged more than 50,000 sessions in a single year. Working together, the people, businesses and institutions of Melbourne are building a future that leverages the city's strengths while working to close the gaps left by past development.

Six Factors, One Method

In these pages, we have outlined six key success Factors that comprise one unified Method for achieving economic development in the digital age, and the social and cultural growth that can both accompany it and give it greater momentum.

Robust, high-quality connectivity opens economic opportunity and creates new pathways for social and cultural progress. The patient work of building a knowledge workforce and innovation-driven economy powers growth in employment, community wealth and competitiveness on the regional, national or even global stage. Taking steps to care for the community through engagement, digital inclusion and sustainability ensures a quality of life that retains and attracts residents and employers, and a resilience that can withstand the climate shocks coming our way.

Setting strategy and taking action in each of these Factors is important. Just as important are the connections and interactions between them. The normal silos of government, businesses and citizens groups are the enemy of progress. It is up to the community's leaders to learn about the many ways that people and organizations are taking action now, and to steer them toward greater collaboration and cooperation. For all the power of technology, nothing substitutes for getting people together over a cup of coffee or tea or a Zoom session and building the relationships on which all progress depends.

Getting Started

The first step is the hardest step: the blank page or empty stage, the welcoming handshake or the opening remarks. Starting Intelligent Community development is challenging because it requires people in government and business to change how they think about the fundamentals of development. It demands that local leaders adopt new priorities. It calls on citizens to accept new costs and benefits and to tolerate uncertainty about outcomes.

The good news – in the words of one Intelligent Community leader – is that it doesn't cost a thing to change your mind. Getting started can be hard, but it does not have to be expensive, and the rewards can be vast.

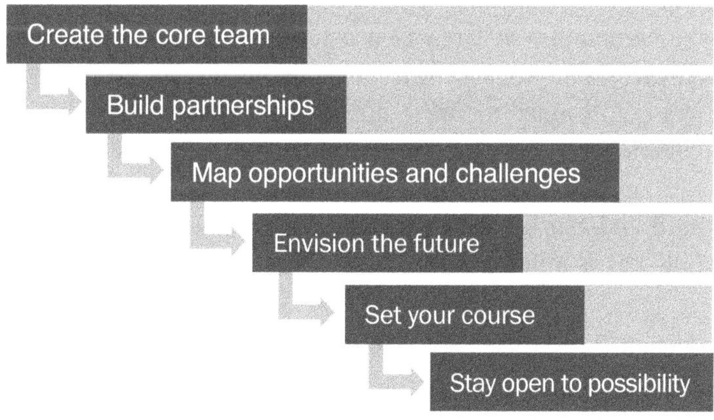

Create your Core Team

No Intelligent Community was ever built overnight or by a single person. Every Intelligent Community begins with a core group of people who decide that the status quo is not working for the community. In most cases, this conviction arises from crisis: the loss of a major employer, natural disaster, social problems from crime to addiction, or what seems unstoppable economic decline and the social disasters it brings. A sense of crisis motivates people to think differently about problems that have long stared them in the face and creates space for new action.

Some remarkable places even embrace change without the sharp prod provided by crisis. In good times, they perceive their risks clearly and embrace action to turn challenge into opportunity. But they are a rarity.

The core team usually takes shape around a community leader – an elected Mayor or leading member of Council. But it can also be led by a businessperson, an educator, a foundation president or a civic leader – anyone recognized by the community at large as a natural leader whose opinions deserve to be heeded. Success as an Intelligent Community requires, sooner or later, the strong commitment of local government, but that commitment does not need be the starting point. Government, by design, acts at a measured pace and can be just as valuable in the role of enthusiastic follower as initial leader.

The core team takes shape from an urgency to address the dangers its members see. Driven by that feeling, they –

- Meet regularly for discussion to build a shared vision of problems to solve and ways to solve them.

- Research what other communities, both near and far, are doing to address similar problems, drawing on information from colleagues, nonprofit (NGO) groups, conferences, the news media and the web. We naturally recommend ICF as a resource.
- Develop the first pass at a SWOT analysis of the community's **strengths**, **weaknesses**, **opportunities** and **threats**, both internal and external, based on the team's knowledge of the community as well as its research.

Build Partnerships

Intelligent Community development is a team sport. Broad and deep collaboration is its essential tool.

Once the core team is united in its mission and vision, it is time to extend the group outward to those who will want to contribute as well as those who may oppose change. The goal is to share the preliminary vision of the core team through –

- One-on-one meetings with those likely to become key stakeholders as well as influential people who may not embrace the vision at first but have the interests of the community at heart.
- Scheduled meetings of natural groupings in the community: economic sectors from tech to finance to property developers, downtown merchants, healthcare providers, public and private educators, arts and culture groups, sports clubs and others.
- A public kick-off event to launch the program.

Many communities have found it useful to establish a formal partnership of people from government, business, education, nonprofits and citizens. The partnership will have a defined scope, regular meetings, sub-groups dedicated to topics and mechanisms for citizen engagement. The partnership helps create credibility for the mission and honors those selected for it.

Where this is not practical, the core team can provide the leadership, provided that it engages frequently with all the key influencers who would participate in a formal partnership.

Whichever approach you take, you must allow time for participants to build trust in the process and in each other.

Groups run on trust, and trust grows one step at a time. You promise to do something and follow through on that promise. I have a need and you connect me with people who can help. Over time, we learn that we can rely on each other's good will. Until trust is established, the group can accomplish nothing of importance, which is why new groups so often fall apart. To avoid that fate, leaders must target simple activities and quick victories in the early stages and tackle the real work of the group when it is ready for the challenge.

Map the Opportunities and Challenges

In the first stage, the core team created a preliminary SWOT analysis of the community. The next priority is to conduct a broader and deeper analysis that engages the partnerships you have created. This is the topic of a series of meetings, either of the full partnership or of sub-groups, which map the strengths and opportunities on the one hand, and the internal weaknesses and external challenges or threats on the other. The ICF Method sets the cardinal directions for that map.

The output of this stage is an Intelligent Community report that presents the vision for change and maps the opportunities and challenges facing the community, with a high-level summary for citizens. This becomes the foundation for the next step.

Envision the Future

With the report as foundation, the next step is to engage the broader community in envisioning its future. Most participants will never read the full report, but its major conclusions in summary form will provide the structure for their work.

This is work that most communities are familiar with: a series of public meetings with representatives from business, institutions and civic groups. Short briefings are followed by brainstorming and small group exercises that draw out hopes, concerns and beliefs about the community's future. Online surveys and digital collaboration tools expand the number of people participating and a strong marketing campaign underlies the entire project. After review and refinement, the core team publishes the results as a set of principles and calls to action that bear the stamp of the citizenry.

Set Your Course

The principles and calls to action provide the basis for planning and execution of the Intelligent Community program. Carrying it out requires the usual mix of milestones and metrics, identification of responsibility and accountability as well as funding for program management and specific initiatives. At this stage, nothing is more important than ensuring that the individual initiatives do not wind up in silos but instead function as interconnected parts of a whole that drive each other's success. This requires continuing leadership at the Council and manager level that sets an example of collaboration across departments.

Stay Open to Possibility

To become an Intelligent Community is to embrace a never-ending wave of change, confident in the community's ability to adapt, learn and make the best of it. While carefully executing approved programs, you must always stay open to new possibilities – many of which will be created by the very programs you are carrying out. These become the basis of new goals and plans, and the cycle of mapping, envisioning and setting your course will need repeating every five to ten years to reflect the changing dynamics of the community.

How Small-to-Midsize Places Can Win in the Decades Ahead

ICF developed its Method with an ambitious goal in mind. We wanted it to be as useful to communities with populations in the hundreds as it is for those in the millions. That's a big challenge, because bigger places have more resources and more people in closer proximity – at least, when public health conditions permit it. They tend to be the dominant economic player across a much greater geographic area.

Those are the very reasons that the digital revolution has so far played to the strengths of big cities, where most tech job growth has taken place. But the same technologies are having another effect, one that is only now becoming visible. Connectivity makes the distance between people and places far less important than it used to be. It allows a company in a small city in New Zealand, for example, to do business all over the world. It brings education from the world's finest institutions to the smallest towns. It empowers places far from the "superstar cities" to develop vibrant local economies, to strengthen their societies and to enrich their cultures for generations to come.

To achieve these things, small places have to work harder, whether they are towns standing alone on the plains or are undervalued neighborhoods in big cities. This is the same work that much bigger places do but at a smaller scale. They need to be smarter and clearer about envisioning a better future. And here, they have an advantage, because they are nimbler, with less bureaucracy and fewer interest groups in competition. As one thought leader in our network put it, there are not too many problems in a small town or neighborhood that can't be worked out face-to-face.

Start Where You Are

When you decide that the status quo is no longer working, your first impulse will be to focus on the negatives. You and your colleagues are frustrated by the loss of employers, the unwillingness of carriers to bring broadband to your community, or the way young people graduate from school and leave town. But most communities have strengths hiding in plain sight that could be leveraged. It might be a municipally owned electric plant that can make a business case for investing in connectivity to improve its operations and extend broadband service at the same time. It might be a cultural festival with the potential to draw visitors from far away if properly marketed online. It might be a school where a few remarkable teachers are training students to work in leading-edge occupations. All these are assets that small Intelligent Communities in our network have leveraged successfully.

Plan for Small Victories

The biggest obstacles to progress for small places are not the facts in front of people's faces but the ideas between their ears. When you are convinced that nothing will change and nothing can be done, your prophecies tend to come true. The best antidote is the small, quick victory that is celebrated as one step on a longer road. Don't be afraid to set inspiring goals but be sure to set many milestones along the way. The milestones need to be more than checkmarks on a to-do list. They need to speak to the needs and concerns of your people.

They should be things that people will want to brag about because they suggest a different and better future for the place called home.

An Obstacle is Just an Invitation to Innovate

There is no shortage of obstacles to the creation of an Intelligent Community. But each one is an invitation to innovate your way around it. Can't get carriers to invest in broadband? Build a network of underground conduit while you work on the roads you own or find a grant to fund wireless towers on public land, where private carriers can hang radios. Don't have a college or university campus? Find an educational partner attracted by something in your community and work to set up a satellite campus, even if it takes years.

In closing, we offer a final set of stories from our network of small-to-midsize communities. They are stories of imagination, determination, willingness to learn from setbacks and relentless faith in a better future. We hope they inspire you to push through your own obstacles and create that future for the place that matters most in all the world: the place called home.

COMMUNITY PROFILE

Stratford, Ontario, Canada

Pop: 31,000 I Top7 Intelligent Community 2013

At the turn of the 21st century, Stratford had a reputation for being quaint, cultured and out of the way, home to the Stratford Shakespeare Festival and a 90-minute drive from Toronto, the business capital of eastern Canada.

The Festival, founded in 1953, is a home-grown success story in cultural tourism. The Fifties were hard times in Stratford, as the prosperity built on agriculture drained away and the national rail system closed its massive maintenance yard. A local journalist named Tom Patterson proposed to Council that he go to New York City and persuade legendary British director Tyrone Guthrie to come to Stratford and create a summer Shakespeare Festival. After all, he reasoned, how could Guthrie resist establishing a summer theater in a town named for Shakespeare's birthplace of Stratford Upon Avon? Improbably, Guthrie did come to Stratford, bringing theater legend (and future Obe Wan Kenobi) Alec Guinness with him, and opened the Festival in a tent near Stratford's Avon River. Today, it is the largest employer in the city and generates hundreds of millions of dollars in local economic activity in ticket sales, restaurants, lodging and culture.

This economic center complemented Stratford's revived industrial base, which supplied the North American automotive and aerospace sectors. But in the late Nineties, the city's forward-looking leadership saw that the growth opportunities of the future would depend on digital communications technology.

A Network for the Shakespeare Festival

Since then, a team led by Mayor Dan Mathieson has executed on an Intelligent Community strategy with great intensity. The city-owned utility has built out a 70-km open access fiber network with a Wi-Fi overlay, and signed sales agreements with commercial carriers to deliver triple-play and mobile services. The network enabled the Festival to significantly expand its online marketing and plays a key role in the city's tourism strategy, which builds on the Festival's reputation to attract "foodies," cyclists and other target groups throughout the year. At the same time, the city has used the network to slash its own telecom costs and power a smart meter program.

Digital Media Campus

After nearly a decade of planning and development, Stratford succeeded in establishing a satellite campus of the University of Waterloo that leverages the presence of an outstanding source of content: the Shakespeare Festival.

Several years went into assembling the components of the deal. It began when city leaders learned that the University was looking for an opportunity to develop a digital media curriculum to add to its career-focused degree programs. Mayor Mathieson proposed Stratford as the ideal location because it was home to the Festival, a ready source of ever-fresh content that would benefit from involving students in developing its digital media capabilities. As negotiations proceeded, the city committed to investing C$10 million to clean up an abandoned industrial site in its downtown core that could serve as a satellite campus. The Province of Ontario matched that investment, as did employers in Waterloo eager to increase the digital media talent pool, and the Federal government added C$5 million. The new building opened in October 2012 to students working in state-of-the-art digital media labs for graphic design, animation, web development and audio and video editing. Two-thirds of them were Canadian, with the remainder coming from other nations.

The school launched with a Masters program in digital media, which is structured to end with internships that lead to employment. It attracts students from arts, engineering and business, deliberately mixing them on interdisciplinary teams that forces them to understand other points of view and to collaborate on projects. They have access to production facilities, digital editing suites and project rooms for highly experiential programs.

The school followed with an undergraduate program, which admitted 93 students from 400 applicants in its first year. The program mixes art, business and technology instruction, with the goal of taking students passionate about art and teaching them business and technology, while exposing business students to the art and technology of digital media. Bundled into the program is project management instruction, so that students emerge with a professional certification in project management.

Creating a Home for Innovation

Having established an institution to produce digital media professionals, Stratford went on to create a home for innovators.

Housed in an historic building downtown, the Stratford Accelerator opened its doors in 2012 with seven clients. It offers housing and advisory services to early-stage tech companies from concept through commercialization. It is an outgrowth of the Waterloo Accelerator Center, which has served 100 companies, of which 50 have graduated and half have stayed in the region, generating an estimated C$80m in revenue. Supporting the companies are five in-house mentors and an entrepreneur-in-residence, who advise on finance, marketing, product development, manufacturing and other fields, as well as helping companies set milestones and execute against them. In addition to long-term relationships with start-ups, the accelerator offers a 3-month program called Pathfinder, which is designed for people with an idea they want to explore but who are not yet ready to devote full time.

With each addition to Stratford's ecosystem, the city's attractiveness to innovators has increased. The economic development team has successfully sold Stratford as a test bed for technology projects – a city large enough to give new technologies a meaningful test but very easy to operate in due to its small size. Toshiba, Cisco, BlackBerry, Inter-Op and Clemson University have all run pilot projects in Stratford. These international brands help validate a strategy that has proven its value.

The near-death of the North American auto industry pushed unemployment in Stratford to 7.9% as the city lost 1,600 mostly low-skilled jobs in manufacturing. But the city also gained hundreds of new jobs requiring ICT skills and saw the revival of automotive create a labor shortage for the higher-skilled manufacturing jobs it retains. For an economy in transition, these trends are a serious validation that it is on the right track.

COMMUNITY PROFILE

Hudson, Ohio, USA

Pop: 22,400 I Top7 Intelligent Community 2020

The 22,000 people of Hudson live in a green stretch of the state of Ohio midway between the cities of Cleveland and Akron.

Despite the major industrial disruptions of the last 40 years, the region is relatively prosperous. Its economy rests on a mix of manufacturing (polymers, automotive, fabricated metals, electrical and electronic parts and aerospace) and services (transportation, health, insurance, banking, finance and retail). Such name-brand companies as Goodyear, Bridgestone, FedEx, Lockheed Martin and JP Morgan Chase have headquarters or major facilities there.

Within the region, Hudson is a prosperous suburban city that provides talent to the region's many employers. Its population is highly educated, with 68% of residents over age 25 holding a bachelor's degree or higher, and relatively young, with a median age of 39. Median household income is in the six figures. Its downtown district is on the National Register of Historic Places. But like Intelligent Communities everywhere, it is a place in transition from one economy to the next. Hudson seeks to secure its future at a time when smaller communities without a distinct competitive advantage are seeing their human, economic and cultural assets drained away by bigger places.

Velocity Broadband

In late 2015, Hudson began construction of the Velocity Broadband Network. That milestone was the end of one journey and the beginning of another. As internet access became essential to businesses, the city began hearing more and more complaints about lack of reliable, affordable connectivity. The largest companies in town could afford dedicated high-capacity service but small-to-midsize companies – the backbone of employment everywhere – could not. A survey of residents and businesses in 2015 made clear that coverage, speed, performance and reliability were a big issue. Some businesspeople reported regularly leaving town for a café with internet access because their own service was so undependable.

The city first tried to interest ISPs in upgrading their infrastructure but the proposals from providers were inadequate and expensive. It pitched potential private-sector partners on buying capacity on an open-access network to be capitalized by the city. The response was tepid. Finally, City Council agreed to become a retail service provider. It made a US$3.3 million internal loan so that its IT department could expand the fiber network that government built for its own use to serve the business community.

Today, Velocity Broadband offers business customers a symmetrical 100x100 Mbps service with capability up to 10 Gbps. More than 150 businesses subscribe to internet service and voice-over-internet-protocol telephone, producing revenues that exceed operating costs. In addition to satisfying existing users, Hudson has seen direct impact on business attraction. For the previous decade, one of the city's primary business parks had only one tenant. Since Velocity Broadband launched, the park has added five new buildings and is close to being fully occupied.

Fire Prevention via Broadband

Hudson's historic downtown is comprised of buildings that are more than 100 years old, many of which are physically attached or at least directly adjacent to one another. Even one building catching fire in the area could spell disaster for downtown, wiping out businesses, lives and history. The primary way to prevent such spreading fires is quick detection, but most options, such as running wires through old brick walls and ceilings, were too expensive for local businesses. The city took advantage of its Velocity Broadband to design a brand-new solution instead.

During the first quarter of 2018, the city coordinated building inspections with the Hudson Fire Department and the Velocity Broadband vendor to check signal strength and determine appropriate locations for wireless fire detection units. These units form a mesh network that communicates back to a central fire panel, allowing Hudson's Fire Department to learn immediately of any fires beginning. In addition, the devices include wireless horn-strobes that alert everyone in the general vicinity to a fire. The city has made historic Main Street a pilot site for this fire detection network with plans to expand if testing goes well.

Center for Innovation and Creativity

An educated population tends to demand much from its educational institutions. In 2010, Hudson was named as one of the 100 Best Communities for Young People by an organization called America's Promise. The award was based on work that began in the 1990s to combat drug use and drive down the dropout rate by enhancing educational and cultural opportunities.

Today, the Hudson City Schools are part of the Six District Compact, a partnership of neighboring school districts, which lets students enroll in two-year higher education programs that earn college credit or provide a pathway directly from high school into employment. Vocational courses range from automotive to cosmetology, and STEM offerings as diverse as coding and robotics lead to the awarding of Microsoft and Cisco certifications.

A 1-to-1 Chromebook program has equipped all students in grades 3-12 with a free laptop, and also paid for a professional Technology Coordinator to manage the project. This mix of technology, training and train-the-trainer programs is a core building block of the knowledge workforce.

Engaging the Community

Hudson's economic development leadership discovered in 2017 that a highly valuable asset was hiding in plain sight. The city is home to nearly 80 Chairs, CEOs and founders of major corporations, universities and nonprofits in the region. To put that talent to work, the city and Hudson Community Foundation established the Business Leader Advisory Board, which meets to prioritize opportunities arising from Velocity Broadband and other developments, and to act throughout the year as advocates for the city beyond its borders.

Another program, Leadership Hudson, introduces its citizen participants to local leaders in government, business and the community, and offers training in leadership. In addition to valuable networking and leadership development, the program offers each class the chance to develop a unique project to benefit the community. In 2014, the Leadership Hudson class partnered with the city-owned electric utility to install a Solar Education Center, complete with solar panels, at the Barlow Community Center. The class raised money for the project from local foundations, businesses and social organizations, as well as a crowdfunding effort that contributed 10% of the total raised. The money went to build a system with 55 roof-mounted and 10 ground-level solar panels, which now provide half the building's electricity and will save the city $100,000 in the next 25 years while reducing carbon emissions by 40 tons per year.

Getting Out of the Way of Progress

City government is making its own contribution to progress by identifying processes that stand in the way of economic growth. The city manager introduced a Continuous Improvement initiative in 2016, and one of its first projects involved the permitting process for residential and commercial construction. It was locally famous for its length and cumbersome procedures: a typical residential application took 11.5 days to process and involved 45 separate steps.

The Continuous Improvement team conducted a week of exhaustive interviews with employees and analyzed the steps in the workflow. At the end of the review, the team proposed to junk the existing software system in favor of a user-friendly online interface that could accept credit cards and \drastically reduced the number of steps. As just one example, residents wanting to add a window or fence to their property typically waited one week for approval by a formal review board. The new system let residents apply for and receive approval without leaving home The residential application requiring 11.5 days and 45 steps was reduced to 2.5 days and 13 steps, and similar gains were made on commercial and industrial applications.

The leaders of Hudson understand the privileges that come with its position as a home for well-educated, well-paid residents working throughout the region. Hudson's citizens already tend to be on the winning side of the transition to a digitally-powered economy – but the city is not one to take its current success for granted. Ambitious programs in broadband, education, economic and community development provide a pathway to a stronger economy and more engaged society for all Hudsonians.

COMMUNITY PROFILE

Nelson, British Columbia, Canada

Pop: 10,500 I Smart21 Community 2017

The city of Nelson has a long history of booming growth, quick modernization, and community action. Founded on the discovery of silver in the nearby mountains, Nelson grew into a thriving transportation and distribution center for the region, expanding its economy into forestry and agriculture as well as mining. The city of just over 10,000 is found in the Selkirk Mountains near the southern border of British Columbia and is the regional seat of the Central Kootenay Regional District, despite making up only about one fifth of the region's population. Nelson has struck a rare balance of modernization and preservation, updating many of its buildings with modern conveniences over the past half century, beginning with aluminum siding in the 1960s, while maintaining its historic downtown as a window into the past.

Broadband Advocacy

Local businesses and organizations can take advantage of Nelson's dark fiber network, Nelson Fibre, which has been in operation since 2005. Nelson Fibre is a growing utility with over 50 fiber strands currently deployed to local businesses, theaters, schools, colleges, municipal departments, and downtown workspaces. The city also has its own local wireless company, Columbia Wireless, which was one of Nelson Fibre's original service providers. To raise awareness of the network, Nelson Fibre issues editorials and press releases to educate key organizations about the benefits of broadband fiber and also about installation and deployment. Columbia Wireless also educates local customers about their internet connectivity options and provides a variety of wireless packages. Thanks to the project, the average business in Nelson knows of the many service providers available in the area.

Nelson's Hackerspace

Founded in 2010 by Brad Pommen, the Nelson Tech Club (NTC) Hackerspace offers weekly technology programs for local youth ages 10-16. The club provides mentors, tools and resources – using a social learning framework based on STEM initiatives – for up to 50 participants each week. NTC provides its tools and resources to the community at low or sometimes no cost to increase technology adoption and train local youth in technical skills for future careers. The club also coordinates with the RoboGames youth robotics competition for the Kootenay region. Since its founding, the NTC Hackerspace has grown into Canada's largest all-ages, public Hackerspace with over 400 registered members.

SMARTS

In addition to broadband services and education, Nelson has also developed programs to help local business and innovators get off the ground. Selkirk-SME Applied Research and Technology Solutions (SMARTS) was developed with Selkirk College to accelerate local small and medium enterprises (SMEs). The SMARTS program helps SMEs develop project plans and secure funding proposals, and also provides access to research support from college faculty and students the areas of geospatial and digital fabrication technologies. Since its creation, the program has aided 38 SMEs and provided 25 other SMEs with references to other organizations when they did not qualify for the program.

Library Access Fills Broadband Gaps

Even with the wide range of broadband services available in Nelson, not all citizens have high-speed internet access. The Nelson Public Library offers access to computers and high-speed

Wi-Fi service, as well as one-to-one training and small group sessions in technology usage. The city provides the public library with 10Mb fiberoptic Wi-Fi service for this purpose.

Path to 2040 Sustainability Plan

Nelson has adapted well to change throughout its history, and to continue this legacy, the city has developed the Path to 2040 Sustainability Plan. As part of this and related plans, the Nelson City Council set aggressive corporate GHG emission targets, resulting in a 25% reduction in corporate emissions to date and making Nelson one of fewer than 10 Canadian municipalities to achieve the highest reduction levels in the Partners for Climate Protection Program. The city has also launched a home energy retrofit program to finance retrofits and a Solar Farm project that has nearly sold out with no subsidies offered.

Nelson has always looked within for strength, from building its own hydroelectric generating system in the early 1900s to the Nelson Fibre network today. By educating its people, connecting them and facilitating local innovation, the city has laid a path toward a future as booming as its past.

COMMUNITY PROFILE

Sunderland, Tyne & Wear, United Kingdom

Pop: 283,700 I Top7 Intelligent Community 2007

Sunderland is not a small place. But its location on the northern border of England and its legacy of hard times qualifies it as one of the places least likely to deserve the name "intelligent."

The largest city in the Northeast of England, Sunderland has quite literally risen from the ashes of the Industrial Age to create a globally competitive city prospering in the Broadband Economy. This transformation was due to neither luck nor location, but to visionary leadership, good planning and unrelenting commitment.

In the 1980s, this former shipbuilding and mining center on the North Sea, which at one time launched more ships than any other port in Europe, had a peak unemployment rate of 22%. As the last shipyard closed in 1988 and the last coal mine followed in 1994, Sunderland fell into the bottom 10% of Britain's "depressed districts." The legacy of heavy industry was a large unemployed group of low-skilled workers, many with chronic health problems. With so little local opportunity, young people fled the city, leaving behind a shrinking and aging population.

Partnership Strategy

Sunderland's government responded in a way that would become a much-copied strategy for success. In 1991, it organized a volunteer group called the Sunderland Partnership, comprised of members from government, local universities, the chamber of commerce and citizen leaders representing important constituencies. The Partnership developed a vision for a new economy based on what Europeans then called "telematics" - the union of telecommunications and computers. While City Council staff labored to translate this vision into measurable goals and meaningful programs, the Partnership focused on politics. Members educated their organizations and constituents about the crisis into which Sunderland had fallen, the challenges to recovery, and their vision for the future. This was to prove essential to Sunderland's success, because it created the political will and integration needed to embrace change.

The Telematics Strategy was published in 1996 to cover a 5-year period through 2001. It included training programs in call center and other digital-age skills for the unemployed, public-access internet kiosks and "electronic village halls" with internet access, business incubation programs and an initial, government-funded high-speed network for the metropolitan area.

Doxford International

Meanwhile, the economic development staff succeeded in persuading a real estate developer to build the first speculative building of what is now Doxford International, an award-winning office park. During the 1990s, it filled and expanded, filled again and expanded again as the European headquarters of Nike and Verisign, and home to such companies as Barclays, CitiFinancial, EDF Energy and T-Mobile. These companies were attracted by the high-quality facilities in a city with attractive wage costs, a strong incentive program, and the availability of freshly trained labor. The same team won public-sector funding from the national government and European Commission and invested it in rebuilding the derelict waterfront into a new home for the University of Sunderland.

By 2000, Sunderland had created 9,000 new jobs. A second Telematics strategy, covering the 1999-2003 period, focused on using ICT to promote social inclusion and ensure that everyone benefited from the city's transformation. It set new goals, including development of a publicly-owned ISP called the Sunderland Host, expansion of the high-speed network to businesses and community centers, and creation of a one-stop Sunderland Portal. There was no let-up, however, in economic development. In 2002, EDS opened its first data center in the North of England in Sunderland. During the three years from 2002 to 2004, Sunderland secured 72% of the new jobs entering the region, despite having just 11% of the North's population.

From 2000 to 2005, the number of net new jobs increased 4.87% compared with the UK average of 3.17%. Sunderland also saw a measurable improvement in the quality of those jobs, with growth primarily in financial and customer services that offered good pay and prospects for advancement. From 2004 to 2005, gross weekly pay in Sunderland rose at three times the national average, and the salary for full-time employees averaged almost double the national minimum.

Working Together

Sunderland's transformation from industrial has-been to Intelligent Community illustrates the power of making many separate elements work in concert. For example, the city's activism about deploying broadband, and willingness to create joint ventures where necessary to reduce risks to the private sector, convinced carriers including NTL-Telewest, BT and Tiscali to provide broadband at competitive costs for speeds up to 10 Mbps. Broadband penetration leaped from 25% to 75% in just two years. The City Council took advantage of this connectivity to create an e-government portal that delivered a wide range of services to about 30,000 visitors per month. Broadband is also the medium for a Virtual Learning Environment created by the City of Sunderland College that is used by more than 20,000 students for training in information technology.

The "electronic village halls" created by the first Telematics Strategy have expanded into multi-agency centers, which provide healthcare, housing, welfare rights, police, job-finder and other services as well youth and sports facilities. Video-conferencing links people using the centers to support staff. These are supplemented by kiosks distributed throughout the city. Sunderland has also identified and trained Community e-Champions to broaden digital inclusion at the neighborhood level, as part of a "peoplefirst" strategy that also equips social service workers with tablets from which they can instantly check databases and record service requests.

Following on the success of Doxford International, Sunderland attracted major investment in technology office parks and incubators. The nonprofit Business & Innovation Center at the Sunderland Science Park offered high-tech workspace that helped create more than 7,000 jobs. The Rainton Bridge Business Park housed incubators and tech facilities and became the site of a 400,000 sq. ft. development by Northern Rock.

The University of Sunderland has become an innovation hub that makes business formation a priority. A Digital Media Center created with support from Sony is the most advanced facility of its kind in the UK, with film, TV and radio studios, and an incubation space for students setting up their own businesses. A New Ventures project facilitates the spin-out of new businesses from research, while the University continues to develop venture financing in collaboration with government and the private sector. A survey revealed that 10% of Sunderland's labor force is self-employed - inspired perhaps by the success of local entrepreneurs like Paul Callaghan, who founded Leighton Group at the Business & Innovation Center in 1997. It is now a global business serving customers including British Airways, Lloyds TSB and Microsoft.

So successful were its efforts to develop a knowledge-based economy that Sunderland began branding itself as the "Software City." It is remarkable to think that, in a single generation, the people of Sunderland moved from slag heaps, slums and stagnation into a future built on turning knowledge into prosperity.

Resources

Detailed reports on the Factors in the ICF Method, illustrated by numerous community examples, are available online: https://www.intelligentcommunity.org/how_to_get_started.

Getting Started
Creating the Intelligent Community

Connecting Your Community
The Digital Infrastructure for Growth

Ladders of Opportunity
Growing and Retaining Tomorrow's Talent

Building the Innovation Ecosystem
How Does Your Garden Grow?

Innovation and the Public Sector

No Neighbor Left Behind
Inclusion in the Intelligent Community

Creating Champions of Change
Engagement for Intelligent Communities

Steering a Sustainable Community

Community Accelerator

In the digital age, communities of every size face new possibilities and new threats. When cities and counties adapt to the demands of the digital age, they survive and thrive amid technology disruption and global competition, regardless of their size or location. Communities that fail to adapt face economic stagnation, decline, population loss and the social and cultural collapse that follows.

ICF's Community Accelerator program empowers communities to tackle these broad possibilities and threats. The Community Accelerator delivers analysis, inspiration and training to help you plan and execute your own vision of an Intelligent Community. It offers a global context for action based on 20 years of experience with cities and regions around the world. More at www.intelligentcommunity.org/accelerator.

Books by ICF

Books by ICF are available from Amazon and on our website at www.intelligentcommunity.org/books.

Brain Gain

How Innovative Cities Create Job Growth in an Age of Disruption

A companion book to *From Connectivity to Community*, *Brain Gain* is a survival manual for cities and regions on how to build economic prosperity and meet social challenges in an age of technological change. It probes the big issues of work and well-being, the innovation economy, offshoring, immigration and the future of big cities and small towns. Innovation and advances in communications technology destroy jobs but also create new ones, cities must decide if they want to take actions that will provide a brain gain or a brain drain.

Seizing Our Destiny

2012's Best Communities to Live, Work, Grow and Prosper In – And How They Got That Way

The story of seven communities that accelerated innovation in business, government and institutions to keep pace with a more innovative world - and offer lessons on how to build political will for change and adapt creatively to the demands of the new century.

Broadband Economies

Creating the Community of the 21st Century

Based on years of research into the best practices of Intelligent Communities, *Broadband Economies* explains the powerful impact of leadership on a community's success and strategies for developing broadband networks, creating a high-skilled workforce, fostering innovation, pursing digital inclusion and building social capital at the local level.

Index

T

U

V

W

Y

Notes

[1] "What in the World is Causing the Retail Meltdown of 2017," by Derek Thompson, *The Atlantic*, April 10, 2017

[2] "Amazon Eats Up 44% of US E-Commerce Sales in 2017," by April Berthene, Internet Retailer, January 8, 2018

[3] "Retail E-commerce Sales Worldwide from 2014 to 2021," Statista, 2019.

[4] "E-Commerce Set for Global Domination – But at Different Speeds," by Michelle Grant. *Forbes*, August 14, 2018.

[5] "The Silent Crisis of Retail Employment," by Derek Thompson, *The Atlantic*, April 28, 2017

[6] "What's Now and Next in Analytics, AI and Automation," McKinsey Global Institute, May 2017

[7] "Giving Young People a Good Start: The Experience of OECD Countries," Norman Bowers, Anne Sonnet and Laura Bardone, OECD Secretariat

[8] "Measuring the Value of Education," by Elka Torpey, US Bureau of Labor Statistics, April 2018.

[9] "Trends in Income and Wealth Inequality," by Juliana Menasce Horowitz, Ruth Igielnik and Rakesh Kochar, Pew Research Center, January 2020. https://www.pewsocialtrends.org/2020/01/09/trends-in-income-and-wealth-inequality/

[10] *Understand How Digital Organizations Evolve to a Digital Business Model*, IDG, 2018 (https://resources.idg.com/download/white-paper/2018-digital-business)

[11] "You'll Be Shocked to Learn How Many Small Businesses Still Don't Have a Website," by Eric Rosenbaum, CNBC, June 2017 (https://www.cnbc.com/2017/06/14/tech-help-wanted-about-half-of-small-businesses-dont-have-a-website.html)

[12] *Global Trends in Renewable Energy Investment*, United Nations Environmental Environment Programme, September 2019.

[13] "Global Markets for Environmental Remediation Technologies," PRNewswire, October 9, 2017.

www.ingramcontent.com/pod-product-compliance
Lightning Source LLC
LaVergne TN
LVHW020643100826
845148LV00012B/2321

* 9 7 8 0 5 7 8 6 9 0 8 9 6 *